Edward Kessler is founder ~~of the Centre~~ for the Study of Jewish–Christian Relations and writes widely on Judaism and Jewish–Christian Relations. Among his many publications is the acclaimed *Bound by the Bible: Jews, Christians and the Sacrifice of Isaac*.

Also available

What Do Muslims Believe? Ziauddin Sardar

What Do **JEWS** Believe?

The Customs and Culture

of Modern Judaism

Edward Kessler

Walker & Company
New York

Published by Walker Publishing Company, Inc., New York
Distributed to the trade by Holtzbrinck Publishers

All papers used by Walker & Company are natural, recyclable products made from wood grown in well-managed forests. The manufacturing processes conform to the environmental regulations of the country of origin.

LIBRARY OF CONGRESS CATALOGING-IN-PUBLICATION DATA
HAS BEEN APPLIED FOR

ISBN-10: 0-8027-1639-3
ISBN-13: 978-0-8027-1639-2

Visit Walker & Company's Web site at www.walkerbooks.com

First published in the United Kingdom by Granta Books in 2006
First U.S. Edition 2007

1 3 5 7 9 10 8 6 4 2

Typeset by M Rules
Printed in the United States of America by Quebecor World Fairfield

For my mother

Contents

Acknowledgements

It is no surprise that writing an introductory work on Jews and Judaism is not an easy task. That it has turned out to be so rewarding is due to a significant number of people.

I would like to thank my editor, Tony Morris, who kept me focused on the task in hand, edited the manuscript with great care and showed patience throughout. I am also grateful to George Miller of *Granta* for his encouragement.

There are a number of other friends and colleagues without whose help this book would not have been completed. I would like to express thanks to my colleagues at the Centre for the Study of Jewish–Christian Relations (CJCR), Melanie Wright, Lucia Faltin, Maty Matyszak, Dan Avasilichioaie and Rachel Davies. Rachel meticulously read the draft chapters and also prepared the chronology and glossary.

The students at CJCR and the Cambridge Theological Federation were, for the most part, a privilege to teach. In fact, teaching is the greatest source of learning and much of the material in this book originated in classes and conversations with my students. Needless to say, any mistakes in the following pages are entirely my own.

My fellow Trustees have always encouraged me to write as well as direct the Centre for the Study of Jewish–Christian

Relations and I am pleased to thank them all – Dominic Fenton, Martin Forward, Bob Glatter, Peter Halban, David Leibowitz, Julius Lipner, Clemens Nathan and John Pickering.

Finally, I would like to acknowledge the support of my family, in particular my wife Trisha and our children Shoshana, Asher and Eliana, who correctly remind me that the priorities of my Jewish life begin at home.

I dedicate this book to my mother whose love and encouragement are unlimited. Since I have included many Jewish stories and sayings in *What Do Jews Believe?* I quote one, which is particularly aposite for my mother:

God could not be everywhere and therefore He made mothers.

1

What does it mean to be a Jew today?

Two Jews were once marooned on a desert island and built three synagogues. Some time later they were rescued by a ship passing by. On the way home the captain asked them why they had built three synagogues. They explained that they had built the first synagogue so that they could pray to God together; they had built the second so that if they argued they could pray in separate synagogues. 'But what was the point of the third?' the captain asked. 'Ah,' they explained, 'we built the third synagogue because we would not go into it.'

Judaism is full of different opinions. In fact, there is no single definition of Judaism that is acceptable to all Jews. Some maintain that Judaism is solely a religion, others that it is a culture, still others emphasize nationhood and attachment with the Land of Israel. And just as there is disagreement about the definition of Judaism, so there is rarely a single agreed Jewish view of any topic. As a general rule, if you are told that all Jews believe x or y, you know the person proposing the view is wrong!

It is, however, possible to outline a picture of Judaism, which gives some sense of the wide variety of views held by Jews. Think of a large family, filled with plenty of tension and disagreement, but a family whose members also love and support one another. Judaism provides its families with many ways to live and is aptly described as a way of life.

This book will examine the Jewish way of life, the expectations of being part of the Jewish family, and the tensions that arise. Sometimes these pressures have resulted in a crisis of the Jewish family and occasionally in violence, one dramatic example being the murder of the Israeli prime minister, Yitzhak Rabin, by a right-wing orthodox Jewish extremist in 1995. The tensions inherent in Judaism include:

- *Secular v. Religious*, illustrated by Isaiah Berlin's comment to Rabbi Jonathan Sacks, 'Please forgive me, Chief Rabbi, for I am a lapsed heretic.'
- *Orthodox v. Progressive*, demonstrated by theological differences over to what extent the *Torah* (The Five Books of Moses) was divinely revealed to Moses.
- *Land of Israel v. Diaspora*, reflected by those Jews who consider Israel their homeland and those who choose to live in another country.

The clearest and most effective way I have found of conceptualizing Judaism is as follows:

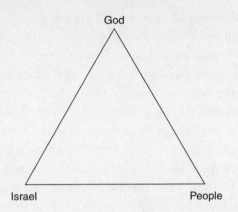

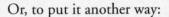

Or, to put it another way:

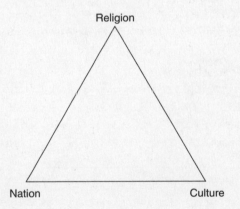

Most Jews can be located in the middle of the triangle, for they possess religious sensibilities, an intimate familiarity with Jewish culture and a strong association with the Land of Israel. Others are located further from the centre. At one tip are ultra-Orthodox Jews who oppose the creation of a Jewish state (which in their view should be created by God or God's anointed, the Messiah) and see no place for culture (except for religious culture) in their lives as Jews.

Another Jewish group located at an extremity of the triangle are those Israelis who are both secular and uninterested in Jewish culture but who identify themselves as Jews in national terms, because of their identification with the State of Israel.

A third group might be defined as those who understand Judaism as the history, culture, ethics and shared experiences of the Jewish people. Their connection to Judaism is not via religious belief or the existence of a Jewish state but rather the combined civilization of an extensive Jewish family.

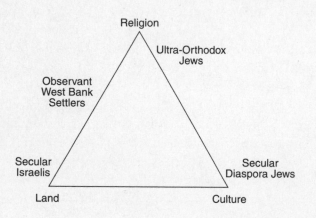

Judaism, therefore, consists of a religion *and* a culture *and* a people. Scholars disagree over the definition of Jewish identity but do, for the most part, accept that Judaism is a mixture of all three elements. This is illustrated by the story of a couple with marital problems who visit their local rabbi to seek his help. The rabbi asks each of them to see him individually. The husband enters the rabbi's study and explains his predicament. The rabbi listens sympathetically and says to him, 'You are right.' The husband leaves. His wife enters the study and explains the problems in their relationship. The rabbi listens carefully, nods his head and when she finishes, says to her, 'You are right.' When the rabbi returns home that evening, he tells his wife what happened. She turns round to him and asks, 'How can they both be right?' The rabbi thinks for a moment and then responds, 'You are right.'

Of course, it is possible to have more than one right answer to a question but in Judaism this approach is commonplace. The *Talmud*, for example, one of the most important collections of Jewish writings from the fifth century CE, sometimes concludes a discussion with the word *teyku* ('let the problem stand') because the rabbis were unable to choose one from a number of answers to a problem so they decided it was better to accept that there could be more than one answer than choose the wrong one. Teyku is an acronym. It stands for *Tishbi yetaretz kushyot v'bayot* ('Elijah will resolve all of our doubts and questions'). The ability to allow for conflicting positions is a feature of Judaism. It is generally posited that the opposite of truth is falsehood: a Jew might suggest that the opposite of one truth may well be another more profound truth.

When the Jewish physicist, Isadore Rabi, won the Nobel Prize for his research, he was asked how he first became interested in science. He explained that his mother made him a scientist without him knowing it. All the other children would come home and their mothers would ask, 'What did you learn at school today?' 'My mother,' he said, used to say, "Izzy, did you ask a good question?"'

Let us begin, therefore, with a question which is more straightforward to answer than 'What does it mean to be a Jew today? and ask what the word 'Jew' means. It comes from the name Judah, a tribe of ancient Israel, which had as its capital Jerusalem. After the ten tribes of Israel were taken into exile by the Assyrians in 721 BCE and were forever lost, Jews were identified as coming principally from the area known as Judaea. Today, scholars number the Jewish people anywhere between twelve and fifteen million people. Part of the reason for the discrepancy is because, as we have seen, there are many different ways to be Jewish. Affiliation to a synagogue, for example, is a poor method of gauging the number. Whatever the exact figure, the total number of Jews today is very small in comparison with other religions (for example, for approximately every hundred Christians, there is only one Jew).

Yet, for a small people whose origins go back some four thousand years – Abraham was thought to have lived in Mesopotamia about 1800 BCE – Judaism has not only survived but also flourished. What is it about Judaism that has given it the ability to last and survive for so long? How has Judaism managed to make such a significant contribution to the religious experience of mankind and to be a major influence on the creation and development of at least two of the world's religions, Christianity and Islam? It is my hope that this book will succeed in answering that question.

Being a minority profoundly affects the ways Jews lead their lives. From biblical times to the modern day, Jews have been aware that they represent but a small percentage of humankind. In the *Mishnah*, a second-century text, the rabbis ask why the Bible begins with Adam and not with Abraham, who is viewed as the father of the Jewish people. They suggest it is to teach that everyone is descended from the same person. 'A single human being was first created for the sake of peace among humanity, so no person can say to another, "my father was greater than yours.'" In other words, the purpose was to emphasize a common humanity.

Being made in the image of God is a feature shared by all people, men and women, black and white, tall and short, weak and strong. Indeed, the Bible makes it clear that even the enemies of Israel – Assyria and Egypt – are to be viewed as having, like Israel, their own special relationship with God. As the prophet Isaiah puts it, 'A blessing be upon Egypt, my people, upon Assyria, the work of my hands, and upon Israel, my possession'. (Isaiah 19:24) We will consider in this book what is understood by the special relationship between Israel and God, the former being sometimes described as the 'chosen people'.

Being a small minority also means that even in Israel, where the majority of citizens are Jewish, there is a strong sense of being surrounded by non-Jews. Often the non-Jewish world has caused much suffering, culminating, for example, in the murder of six million Jews in the Second World War. The existence of anti-Semitism and the horrors of the Holocaust have had a deep impression on Judaism (and Christianity), which continues to this day. One consequence of being a small minority has, therefore, been a sense that the outside world is a threat.

At its root, anti-Semitism is fuelled by the rejection of humane, moral values. As Anne Frank, the Jewish schoolgirl in hiding from the Nazis in occupied Amsterdam, wrote in her diary, 'If we bear all this suffering and if there are still Jews left when it is over, then Jews, instead of being doomed, will be held up as an example. Who knows, it might even be our religion from which the world and all peoples learn good, and for that reason only do we now suffer.'

There is, of course, the possibility that emphasizing the Holocaust leads to a loss of perspective. Jewish philosopher Emil Fackenheim proclaimed that the Holocaust resulted in a new commandment (the 614th, since traditionally there are 613 biblical commands), which stressed that it was incumbent upon Jews to survive as Jews. According to Fackenheim one remained a Jew so as not to provide Hitler with a posthumous victory. However, if Jewish identity becomes Holocaust-centred, Jews (and non-Jews) will gain a distorted view. Constructing a negative Jewish identity and omitting the positive side of Judaism will not benefit future generations.

A more positive consequence of being a minority has been a high level of sensitivity to the plight of others and especially a concern for the more vulnerable. A command in the Torah is to 'love thy neighbour as thyself'. The Torah further commands Jews on thirty-six separate occasions to 'love the stranger' because 'you were strangers in the land of Egypt'. The Bible, and the later rabbinic writings, depict God as taking special care of the vulnerable. On some occasions, as recorded in the Book of Psalms, David calls on God to arise and scatter his enemies, yet there is no mention in the Psalms that God responds. The Psalms do, however, state: 'For the oppression of the poor and the cry of the needy, then will I arise, saith the Lord.' This brings to mind the comment attributed to Abraham Lincoln when asked on the eve of battle whether God was on his side. 'The question,' Lincoln is reported to have replied, 'is whether we are on God's side.'

Even if you are God's anointed, even King David, you may not assume that God is on your side. When is God on your side? When you are on his. And what is his side? It is above all the side of the needy and vulnerable; and the extent to which all peoples address themselves to these concerns is, according to the Jewish way of life, the extent to which they are godly.

2

Who are Jews today?

Thus saith the LORD of hosts, the God of Israel, unto all the captivity, whom I have caused to be carried away captive from Jerusalem unto Babylon: Build ye houses, and dwell in them, and plant gardens, and eat the fruit of them; take ye wives, and beget sons and daughters; and take wives for your sons, and give your daughters to husbands, that they may bear sons and daughters; and multiply ye there, and be not diminished. And seek the peace of the city whither I have caused you to be carried away captive, and pray unto the LORD for it; for in the peace thereof shall ye have peace.

(Jeremiah 29:4–7)

Countries with the largest Jewish population

United States of America	5,950,000
Israel	5,100,000
Russia	717,000
France	607,000
Argentina	395,000

Canada	394,000
United Kingdom	302,000
Ukraine	142,000
Germany	107,000
Brazil	95,000
Australia	90,000
South Africa	89,000
Belarus	72,000
Hungary	60,000
Mexico	53,000
Belgium	52,000
Spain	48,000
Netherlands	33,000
Moldova	31,000
Uruguay	31,000
Italy	30,000
Venezuela	25,000
Poland	25,000
Chile	21,000
Iran	20,000

Source: US State Department's *International Religious Freedom Report 2004*

Cities with the largest Jewish population in the Diaspora

New York	1,750,000
Miami	535,000
Los Angeles	490,000
Paris	350,000
Philadelphia	254,000
Chicago	248,000
San Francisco	210,000
Boston	208,000
Moscow	200,000
London	200,000

Source: World Jewish Congress 2003

Cities with the largest Jewish population in Israel

Jerusalem	690,000
Tel Aviv-Jaffa	365,000
Haifa	270,000
Rishon LeZiyyon	215,000
Ashdod	192,000
Beersheva	183,000

Source: Israel Central Bureau of Statistics 2003

AN EXPLANATION OF THE STATISTICS

There are many estimates of the total number of Jews in the world. Most suggest a figure of between 12 and 15 million, which is growing by an estimated 0.3% per annum (compared to a total world population growth rate of 1.4%, 0.1% in more developed countries). The figures I have provided are based on the research of the World Jewish Congress (WJC), according to which 80% percent of Jews live in two countries, the United States of America and Israel, and 95% are concentrated in ten countries. There is not a single Diaspora country where Jews amount to 25 per 1,000 (2.5%) of the total population and only three Diaspora countries have more than 1% of Jews in their total population. In relative terms, therefore, Jews are thinly scattered nearly everywhere in the Diaspora.

After the Holocaust and the end of the Second World War, the Jewish population grew by approximately 1.1 million, followed by growths of 500,000 in the 1960s, 235,000 in the 1970s, 50,000 in the 1980s, and 340,000 in the 1990s. The growth of the 1990s reflects cases of individuals entering Judaism, especially from Eastern Europe, as well as a short-lived 'echo effect' of the post-war 'baby boom'.

In the State of Israel, the Jewish majority amounts to 772 per 1,000 (77.2%) − including the 208,000 Jews but not the Arab population of the Palestinian National Authority and other administered areas. Jews represent 8.5% of the total population in the West Bank.

Israel's population is 6.78 million, of whom 5,180,000 are Jewish. Of these, 66% were born in Israel, and 34% were born abroad. In 1948, those numbers were almost exactly reversed. Jerusalem is the largest city but most of Israel's population is located in the centre of the country around Tel Aviv. Beersheva is the largest city in the south and Haifa the largest in the north.

30% of Israel's population, or 1.5 million people, were born in Israel to a family in which the father was born in Israel, and 1.2 million people were born in Israel to a father born in the former Soviet Union. Morocco is the country of origin of about 500,000 Israelis and 245,000 are from Iraq.

To understand the geographical shape of the Jewish world it is necessary first to appreciate the relationship between Jews who live in the Land of Israel and those who live outside. The latter are described as living in the Diaspora, a Greek word meaning 'scattering', or in the *Galut*, a Hebrew word meaning 'exile'.

Thus, there is a tension between the view that Jews outside of Israel live in Diaspora (a voluntary situation desirable to the individual) or in Galut (an undesirable situation). Galut is understood as a divine punishment, whereas Diaspora existence indicates a positive role for the Jewish people among the nations of the world.

The exodus of Jews from their original homeland had already begun in biblical times. The destruction of the northern kingdom of Israel by Assyria in 721 BCE led to the scattering of the Ten Tribes of Israel. Some went to Egypt; but the first major Diaspora community to flourish was in Babylon, shortly before the destruction of the First Temple in 586 BCE. This was the first of two Temples in Jerusalem to be destroyed. The Second Temple was destroyed by the Romans in 70 CE, and led to the dispersion of the Jews throughout the Diaspora.

Yielding to political authority was a strategy that contributed both to the survival and also to the success of Jewish life. By relinquishing desire for sovereignty, Jews gained autonomy in regulating their lives. Under the motto *dina d'malkulta dina* ('the law of the land is the law') the Jewish community based its existence on the law of a particular host society. The Babylonian experience epitomized this. From then on a large-scale Jewish Diaspora developed in Greek-speaking countries and throughout the Roman Empire. In fact, well before the destruction of the Second Temple (70 CE), more Jews lived in the Diaspora than in Israel.

By and large, therefore, Jews chose to lead their lives outside Israel. At the same time, they affirmed their connection by praying towards Jerusalem, asking God for the end of the exile and for a return to Israel. Other traditions, such as the custom of breaking a glass at a wedding and leaving a wall undecorated in the home, reminded Jews of the Land left behind.

The system worked. For hundreds of years Jews lived comfortably in distant lands while also looking forward to a return to their ancient homeland. As Jeremiah wrote, 'He that scattered Israel will gather him and keep him, as a shepherd his flock' (Jeremiah 29:10). Where Jews suffered oppression, they mourned their land more actively and prayed for the messianic era to be initiated by God, an era that would bring them back to Israel. This is illustrated by the following story in the Talmud:

> Wherever Israel went into exile, the Shechina [God's presence] went along into exile. They went to exile to Egypt, the Shechina went with them . . . They went to Babylon in exile and the Shechina went with them . . . And when they will eventually be redeemed, the Shechina will be redeemed along with them.
>
> (Megillah 29a)

The name *Shechina* represents the feminine aspect of God and is understood as 'God's Presence'. The story indicates that alongside the hope of divine restoration there existed the mystical idea that God was also exiled with His people. Wherever Jews live, God was with them. Just as Jews suffered in exile so God suffered with them, demonstrating that God cared particularly for the vulnerable. And just as Jews needed to be redeemed, so one aspect of God also needed redemption!

This belief helped Jews survive, particularly during periods of oppression, and generated messianic hopes of redemption. The Promised Land became a symbol of redress for all the wrongs Jews had suffered.

Jewish suffering and oppression continued for many centuries, from the massacres of Jews during the crusades, to the expulsion of Jews from many European countries during the fifteenth and sixteenth centuries, and the pogroms of the nineteenth and twentieth centuries.

In the late nineteenth century, Jews took their destiny into their own hands and stopped waiting for divine intervention. This was a dramatic break from the traditional Diaspora survival strategy, illustrated by the rabbinic saying, 'a person must be at all times yielding like a reed and not unbending like a cedar'. (Ta'anit 20a) After hundreds of years of persecution, particularly in Christian lands, Jews began to abandon the traditional teaching, which suggested that if only Jews were faithful, God would eventually bring them and their families back to Jerusalem. From the 1880s onwards, Jews began actively to migrate back to the Land of Israel, then part of the Ottoman Empire. The horror of the years 1933–45 was interpreted as the ultimate demonstration of the inadequacy of passive waiting. It was argued that if the State of Israel had come into existence twenty years earlier (than 1948), it might have saved European Jewry from destruction. For many Jews, therefore, the Jewish state offered not only the possibility of religious and cultural fulfilment but also the best hope for survival.

Martin Buber, an early twentieth-century Jewish philosopher, explained the Jewish historical attachment to the Land of Israel in a letter to Mahatma Gandhi, written in response to Gandhi's criticism of Zionism, the Jewish movement to reestablish a homeland in the Land of Israel. Gandhi had recommended that Jews remain in Germany and pursue *satyagraha* ('holding on to truth', the basis for his non-violent resistance to British rule) even unto death. Buber rejected this argument and explained the connection between the Jewish people and the land as follows:

> You say, Mahatma Gandhi, that a sanction is 'sought in the Bible' to support the cry for a national home, which 'does not make much appeal to you'. No, this is not so. We do not open the Bible and seek sanction there. The opposite is true: the promises of return, of reestablishment, which have nourished the yearning hope of hundreds of generations, give those of today an elementary stimulus, recognised by few in its full meaning but effective also in the lives of many who do not believe in the message of the Bible.
>
> (*The Letters of Martin Buber* ed.,
> N.N. Glatzer and P. Mendes-Flohr, 1991,
> NY: Schocken pp. 479–80)

Before the Holocaust not all Jews supported a Jewish state. Indeed, Zionism led to vociferous arguments between Jews, secular and religious, Reform and Orthodox. For example, some Jews rejected the concept of a Jewish state by arguing that Israel should be a divine and not a man-made creation (a view still held by some in the ultra-Orthodox tradition); some Reform Jews emphasized universal values and rejected any form of Jewish nationalism.

I will discuss the significance to Jews of the State of Israel later in this book, but it is worth pointing out now that whereas the early Zionists viewed themselves as superior to Jews in the Galut, in the last quarter-century attitudes have changed, particularly as Jews in the West have begun to recover confidence after the Holocaust. For Diaspora Jews there has developed a strong sense of belonging and of being at home: for many, the Promised Land is where they are, not in the Land of Israel. They consider themselves very strongly to be in Diaspora, not in the Galut.

Moreover, they support Israel either financially, socially (by visiting the country), or politically (lobbying on Israel's behalf). Thus, the relationship between Israel and the Diaspora today seems more balanced. Just as there had been two Jewish centres coexisting side by side in Babylon and Israel in the Talmudic period (third to fifth or sixth century CE), so a flourishing Jewish life exists both in Israel and the Diaspora, particularly in the United States of America. There are indications that, perhaps for the first time in Jewish history, a true dialogue between Israeli and Diaspora Jews is developing. It is certainly very much needed.

3

How did we get here?

Four Snapshots of Jewish History

Abraham to Moses
The Rabbinic Period
Anti-Semitism and the Holocaust
Zionism and the Creation of the State of Israel

Abraham to Moses

Abram tried to convince his father, Terach, of the folly of idol worship. One day, when Abram was left alone, he took a hammer and smashed all of the idols in his father's house except the largest one. He placed the hammer in the hand of this idol. When his father returned and asked what happened, Abram said, 'The idols began to fight each other, and the biggest smashed all the others.' His father said, 'Don't be ridiculous. These idols have no life or power. They can't do anything.' Abram replied, 'Then why do you worship them?'

(Midrash Genesis Rabbah)

Judaism begins with Abraham, initially called Abram, born in Ur, Babylonia, who came to realize that the universe was the work of a single Creator. The Bible recounts how God commanded Abram to leave his home and his family, and how God blessed him and said he would make a great nation of his children. God thus established a *b'rit* ('covenant') with Abram and, by extension, with the Jewish people. Covenant is a thread that runs through Jewish history, involving rights and duties on both sides: just as we have certain obligations to God, so, Jews believe, God has certain obligations to us.

Abram was worried that he had no children, so his wife Sarai offered her maidservant, Hagar, as a concubine. She bore Abram a son, Ishmael, who, according to both Muslim and Jewish tradition, is the ancestor of the Arabs. When Abram was 100 and Sarai 90, God again promised Abram a son, and Abram took on a new name, Abraham ('father of many'), while Sarai became Sarah ('princess'). Isaac was born and God's promise to Abraham began to be fulfilled.

Isaac is best known for his role in one of the most terrifying stories of the Bible – the Binding of Isaac, where Abraham is asked by God to sacrifice his son, Isaac. (Genesis 22) This tale is similarly depicted in Islam, except that Ishmael, rather than Isaac, is viewed as the son Abraham wishes to sacrifice. The theme of the story is Abraham's relationship with God and how his faith in, and commitment to God, was demonstrated by his willingness to sacrifice his long-awaited son at God's command.

As a piece of writing, the biblical account seems to have everything. It has enough action, tension and drama for a five-act play, yet it is compressed into a mere eighteen verses. It is packed with energy and dynamism. It arouses both terror and pity. It deals with the biggest of themes and touches the deepest of emotions. And it seems to have a happy ending.

Only one ingredient is missing – an immediately apparent, morally acceptable and topically relevant message. How could Abraham reconcile the bizarre demand by God to sacrifice his son against the divine promise that he would be the ancestor of a people who would spread throughout the world? Woody Allen writes:

> . . . but at the last minute the Lord stayed Abraham's hand and said, 'How could thou doest such a thing?'
> And Abraham said, 'But thou said . . .'
> 'Never mind what I said,' the Lord spake. 'Dost thou listen to every crazy idea that comes thy way?'
> And Abraham grew ashamed. 'Er – not really . . . no.'
> 'I jokingly suggest thou sacrifice Isaac and thou immediately runs out to do it.'
> And Abraham fell to his knees. 'See, I never know when you're kidding.'
> And the Lord thundered, 'No sense of humour. I can't believe it.'
> 'But doth this not prove I love thee, that I was willing to donate mine only son on thy whim?'
> And the Lord said, 'It proves that some will follow any order, no matter how asinine, as long as it comes from a resonant, well-modulated voice.'

Over the years Jewish commentators have tried to make sense of this story, offering a variety of interpretations from the traditional view that Abraham offered a model response to the divine command to the postmodern view that he failed the test because God wanted him to reject the command. In my view, we should simply conclude, teyku, meaning let the matter stand, and allow conflicting interpretations of this terrifying story.

Isaac married Rebecca and she became pregnant with twins.

God told her that her two sons would become two nations and the older would serve the younger. She had a difficult pregnancy. The two brothers, Esau and Jacob, fought each other even before they were born. Esau was Isaac's favourite, because he was a good hunter, but the more spiritually minded Jacob was Rebecca's favourite. When Isaac was growing old, Rebecca tricked him into giving Jacob a blessing meant for Esau. Jacob then fled to live with his uncle, where he met a woman called Rachel. Jacob was deceived into marrying Rachel's older sister, Leah, but later married Rachel as well, together with Rachel and Leah's maidservants, Bilhah and Zilpah. Between these four women, Jacob fathered twelve sons (the ancestors of the tribes of Israel) and one daughter (Dinah).

After many years, Jacob sought reconciliation with Esau. The night before they were due to meet, he wrestled until dawn with a mysterious man, who eventually revealed himself as an angel and blessed Jacob, giving him the name Israel meaning 'the one who wrestled with God'. The term 'Children of Israel' signifies descent from Jacob and is applied to all Jews. The next day, 'Esau ran to meet him, and embraced him, and fell on his neck, and kissed him: and they wept.' (Genesis 33:4)

Along with the patriarchs, Abraham, Isaac and Jacob, and the matriarchs, Sarah, Rebecca, Rachel and Leah, it is the figure of the prophet Moses who dominates the Torah. Moses led the Israelites out of slavery in Egypt, and guided them for forty years in the wilderness. During this time, he brought down the Ten Commandments from God on Mount Sinai, and prepared the entry of the Children of Israel into the land of Canaan before dying at the age of 120 without ever entering the Promised Land.

Moses was born at a time when the Pharaoh of Egypt had decreed that all male Hebrew infants were to be drowned at birth. Miriam, Moses' older sister, who was also a prophet,

ensured his survival as a baby, by leaving him in a basket float-
ing on the river. When Pharaoh's daughter walked by and heard
the crying child, she adopted him. It is no coincidence that the
future liberator of the Israelites was raised as an Egyptian prince.

As a young man, outraged at seeing an Egyptian overseer
beating an Israelite slave, Moses killed the overseer and fled to
the land of Midian where he married Tzipporah, one of the
Midianite priest's daughters, and became the shepherd for his
father-in-law's flock. One day, while out tending his sheep,
Moses saw a bush that was burning but without being con-
sumed and heard the voice of God, who commanded him to
return to Egypt and with his brother, Aaron, make one simple
if revolutionary demand of Pharaoh: 'Let my people go.'

As well as leading the Children of Israel from slavery to freedom – see the poem below – Moses received a further divine
revelation on Mount Sinai. He went on to impress his
monotheistic vision upon Judaism with such force that in the
succeeding three millennia Jews have never confused the mes-
senger with the author of the message.

The story of the Exodus from Egypt is recounted at the
Passover meal. In my family we include a poetical account such as
the following written by Martin Singer from Exeter Synagogue:

From Abraham to Moses in rhyme

It started with Abraham, who made the news
By becoming the very first of the Jews.
He had a wife called Sarah and a 'friend' as well
Who gave him a son called Ishmael.

Sarah was quite old and getting dizzy
But to everyone's surprise had a son called Izzy

(His name was Isaac but Izzy will do)
And he became the very next Jew.

Izzy met Rebecca and lost his head
So he asked the question and they soon got wed.
They had two sons for goodness sake
And called one Esau and the other Jake.

Izzy hoped that Esau could be a sensation,
As the one to found the Jewish Nation.
But in confusion he didn't know whom to choose
So Jacob became the next of Jews.

Jacob worked for seven years just to get wed,
Thought he'd marry Rachel but got Leah instead.
For Rachel he worked for seven years more,
(don't trust your bosses, that's for sure).

Jake's youngest sons he loved more than the rest,
Benjamin and Joseph who was a real pest.
He translated dreams and told others that he
Would soon be just like royalty.

Joseph's brothers could take no more,
They wanted him away for sure,
So when they saw some merchants they gave a wave
And sold poor Joseph to be a slave.

But Joseph was a bit too clever for that,
For in Egypt he became a diplomat.
He persuaded the farmers to store their food
As he knew the good weather would change its mood.

When the famine came there were no fears,
Everyone had prepared for years.
But the brothers were hungry and getting thin,
No food in the fridge, no bread in the bin.

So they went to see their brother Jake,
To get some food and a piece of cake.
They said, 'Help us our plate is empty';
Jake invited them to live in the land of plenty.

In Israel the crops all withered and died,
But living in Egypt the Jewish people multiplied.
Years later there came a new Pharaoh,
And of the family of Jacob, he did not know.

He said, 'Who are these terrible Jews?
They eat our food and use our loos.
This is wrong, make them work for less,
And build me a palace at Ramases.'

A boy was born to a Jewish wife
And she was determined to save his life.
She made a basket that would float,
And put Moses on the river just like a boat.

Moses grew up to care for the sheep
A peaceful job he'd like to keep.
He enjoyed his life, didn't like to rush,
And then he saw a burning bush.

Although the bush was well on fire,
The flames seemed to get no higher.

The bush survived the flames just fine;
Moses decided this was a sign.

He had to go and save his fellow Jews
There really was no time to lose!
He had to go and make it snappy,
His countrymen were really quite unhappy.

Moses' brother knew a few neat tricks
That might put Pharaoh in a fix,
But when Moses said, 'Let my people go',
Pharaoh just smiled and replied NO.

Moses said, 'We'll turn the rivers to blood',
Pharaoh didn't believe he could.
Then on the day the water turned red,
Pharaoh changed his mind instead.

Moses said, 'I've sent nine plagues,
You've not changed even one of your ways.
Now your last chance has come and gone
Tonight will die your only son.'

Moses went to Pharaoh who dried his eyes
He said, 'Don't wait for your bread to rise,
Don't eat breakfast or have a shower,
Take your people and go within the hour.'

They took all they could and became free,
And ran all the way to the Red Sea.
But Pharaoh sent his army to follow them
As he had changed his mind again.

They went to the sea and they passed through it
Pharaoh's army chased them, you just knew it
But the sea wouldn't stay and his soldiers were drowned
The Jews walked free but then they found

As Moses led them back to the Promised Land
Across the sea and across the sand
They had to walk for forty years more
And were ordered around like slaves as they were before!

http://www.members.fortunecity.com/exetershul/newsletter/
poemspassover.html

The Rabbinic Period

Once there was a Gentile who came to Rabbi Shammai, and
said, 'Convert me on the condition that you teach me the whole
Torah while I stand on one foot.' Shammai rejected him. The
man then came to Rabbi Hillel, who converted him, saying,
'Do not do unto others as you would not wish to be done to
yourself; this is the whole Torah. The rest is commentary, go
and learn it.'

(Talmud, Shabbat 31)

The first major challenge faced by Jews in the post-biblical period
was the destruction of the Second Temple by the Romans in
70 CE. The Temple at Jerusalem had been the centre of Jewish
religious life. Its demolition, followed sixty-five years later by the
expulsion of Jews from the city, was a serious threat to the survival
of Judaism. In fact only two Jewish groups survived its destruction: rabbinic Jews and Jewish followers of Jesus.

It is unclear when the so-called 'rabbinic period' in Jewish history began. Perhaps it started as early as the fifth century BCE, with the return to Jerusalem of Nehemiah and Ezra, or as late as the second century BCE during the Hasmonean dynasty. What is certain is that the rabbinic way of life was a new stage in the development of Judaism and enabled Jews to survive without a homeland as well as without a temple. It was the rabbis' ability to respond to the new situation that enabled them, eventually, to dominate Jewish life for the next 1,800 years.

There were many different Jewish groups in the first century: Pharisees, Sadducees, Essenes, Hellenizers, Zealots and the followers of Jesus. In contrast with the Zealots, who concentrated on the removal of foreigners (be they Romans or Greeks) from Jewish soil, the Pharisees (who later became known as the rabbis), emphasized study of the Torah and its application in *Halakhah* (Jewish law). They developed an Oral Torah, consisting of comments and explanations on and alongside the Written Torah, the Pentateuch. This oral expression was codified and written down many centuries later in the Talmud. The Pharisees also maintained a belief in the afterlife, described a Messiah whose arrival would herald an era of world peace, and emphasized the importance of individual and communal prayer.

The Sadducees were the Temple-centred aristocracy, who wanted to maintain the priestly caste, but were also willing, like the Hellenizers, to incorporate Greek culture into their lives, something which the Pharisees opposed. The Sadducees rejected the idea of the Oral Torah and insisted on a more literal interpretation of the Written Torah. Consequently, they did not believe in an afterlife, since it is not mentioned in the Torah. Their main concern was Temple ritual. It is no surprise, therefore, that they disappeared after its destruction.

A third group, the Essenes, consisted of desert-based monastic orders that believed that the Temple had been corrupted by other Jewish groups. They were ascetics who adopted strict dietary laws and maintained a celibate life. One group of Essenes lived near the Dead Sea where, in 1947, a Bedouin shepherd discovered manuscripts, which came to be known as the Dead Sea Scrolls. These described their beliefs as well as events of the time. He also discovered the earliest known copies of the Bible.

The Jewish followers of Jesus were the other Jewish sect who survived the destruction of the Temple. Jesus was obviously a Jew (although one of my students once suggested that his mother was Catholic) who followed Jewish customs such as the dietary laws, prayed in the Temple and was called a rabbi. The Christians rivalled the rabbis in their search for adherents to their teachings. The date of the split between Judaism and Christianity has been the subject of much debate. Some suggest it began as early as Paul of Tarsus (around 60 CE), others as late as Constantine (around 300 CE), or even later. One scholar, James Dunn, has sensibly described the separation in terms of a *series* of 'partings of the ways'.

The rabbis replaced pilgrimage to the Temple with prayer, study of the scripture, and works of piety, thereby eliminating the need for a sanctuary in Jerusalem and making Judaism a religion capable of fulfilment anywhere. Contemporary Judaism is ultimately derived from the rabbinic movement of the first centuries. As a result of their endeavours, Jews have often been called 'the people of the Book', although a more accurate description might be 'people of the books' for there are many sacred books. Constant study is one of the prime obligations of religious Jews. Indeed, secular Jews also acknowledge the centrality of the Jewish literary tradition in their practice.

The Jewish books begin with the Bible, continue through the associated legal and homiletical literature and extend to medieval codes, philosophical works and the literature of the mystics. In addition, every area of this vast literary corpus is complemented by detailed commentaries and annotations. Thus, rabbinic emphasis on study resulted in a huge number of works so that if today you read the Bible or the Talmud you read it alongside the interpretations of generations of rabbis.

Hebrew is the language of almost all the Hebrew Scriptures. Towards the end of the biblical period, Jews in the Land of Israel spoke Aramaic but prayed in Hebrew, which remained solely a language for prayer and study for all Jews until in recent times it was revived as a spoken language in Israel.

The foundation of all Jewish writings is the Torah, which in its narrowest sense refers solely to the Pentateuch, or Five Books of Moses. For traditional Jews, the Torah is viewed as the literal word of God and is the object of continual study and interpretation. They are enjoined to 'turn the Torah over and over again, for everything is in it. Contemplate it and grow old and grey over it.' (Ethics of the Fathers 5:25) This study takes place in a *yeshiva*, a Jewish school of learning.

The rabbis, who were respected teachers and scholars, felt it was their duty to explore and expound the divine truth and to live their lives in accordance with the divine will. Their exploration is exemplified by a type of Jewish literature called *midrash* (meaning 'search' or 'enquiry'), in which the rabbis expounded the text, word by word, deriving ethical precepts or messianic expectations from the biblical stories.

Today midrash has the nuance of 'exposition'. It suggests the rabbis' attempt to fill in the gaps of meaning and to elucidate scripture where its meaning seems to be ambiguous. The purpose of their interpretations is to uncover what has always been there, but was previously unseen or undiscovered. There are, in midrash, no wrong interpretations. Yet, on some questions, it is possible to detect a general thrust sufficient for certain conclusions to be drawn as broad principles, always provided that confident assertion is tempered with a healthy degree of scepticism.

Side by side with the development of midrash, great teaching academies created another type of literature which was also bound up with the desire to discover the will of God – the Talmud (literally meaning 'learning' or 'study'), which consists primarily of debates about and discussions of God's laws, as expressed in the Torah. Any attempt to lead a life in accordance with biblical precept faces difficulties caused by gaps in the biblical narrative or uncertainty over the meaning of certain terms. For example, the Bible states that 'no manner of work' should be done on the Sabbath – but what exactly is meant by work? The Talmud tries to answer this and similar questions.

Two of the most famous rabbis are Hillel and Shammai, who lived during the reign of King Herod (37–4 BCE), an oppressive period in Jewish history because of the Roman occupation of Palestine. Shammai was concerned that if Jews had too much contact with the Romans, Judaism would be weakened, and this attitude was reflected in his strict interpretation of Jewish law. Hillel did not share Shammai's fear and was more liberal in his views, being more lenient, for example, in his acceptance of converts to Judaism. Interestingly, Judaism has never exhibited missionary tendencies, unlike Christianity and Islam. This may have been the result of its minority status in Christian and Muslim countries, but may also have resulted from its emphasis on right action rather than right belief.

The disciples of Hillel and Shammai were often in conflict. The Talmud records over three hundred differences of opinion between them, some of which even ended in fights. The regular disagreement is illustrated by the following more modern story.

A London yeshiva decided to field a crew of rowers in a regatta. Unfortunately, they lost race after race. They practised for hours every day, but never managed to come in any better than last. The Principal finally decided to send one of them to spy on the Cambridge University team. So he travelled to Cambridge and hid in the bulrushes off the River Cam, from where he carefully watched the Cambridge team as they practised. He returned to the yeshiva and said, 'I have figured out their secret. They have eight men rowing and only one shouting.'

Anti-Semitism and the Holocaust

In the 1930s a Jew is travelling on a bus in London, reading *The Jewish Chronicle*. Suddenly, to his shock, he spots a friend of his reading a Nazi newspaper. He glares at his friend in anger. 'How can you read that Nazi filth?' he asks. Unabashed, his friend looks at him. 'So what are you reading, *The Jewish Chronicle*? And what do you read there? In England there is an economic depression and Jews are assimilating. In Palestine, Arabs are rioting and Jews are being killed. In Germany they have taken away all our legal rights. You sit there and read all about it, and get more and more depressed. I read the Nazi newspaper. We own all the banks and control all the governments.'

From slavery in Egypt through to the concentration camps and the Holocaust there has not been a time when Jews have not had to think deeply about the problem of suffering as they encountered it in their own lives. Each generation of Jews has a story to tell about facing anti-Judaism and in more recent centuries, anti-Semitism. Anti-Judaism refers to the pre-Enlightenment theological denigration of Judaism. Anti-Semitism refers to hatred of Jews since the Enlightenment, rooted in theories of 'scientific racism' and cultural mistrust. Recent forms of anti-Semitism have appeared in the guise of extreme anti-Zionism, neo-Nazism and in radical forms of Islam.

Some scholars trace anti-Jewish polemic to the New Testament but others suggest the arguments described there are more a reflection of deep internal disputes *within* Judaism. Whatever the origins, anti-Judaism became incorporated into mainstream Christian theology from early on. The Church Fathers, for example, taught that Jews had been replaced by Christians as God's people. Such teachings sowed the seeds for anti-Jewish attitudes that came to dominate Christian thinking from the fourth to the twentieth century: Jewish suffering was a divine punishment for the death of Jesus and the rejection of Christianity.

The position of Jews under Islam was quite different. Despite a subordinate status in Muslim society, Jews were granted security, freedom of worship and a large measure of self-government. For these reasons Judaism flourished more under Muslim than Christian rule.

In Christendom, during the medieval period in particular, Jews were viewed as satanic figures, and Christians felt free to attack them with a divine seal of approval. There were outbreaks of tolerance during many bleak centuries, such as the Golden Age in medieval Spain around 1000 CE when a relatively peaceful coexistence between Jews, Christians and Muslims prevailed and Jews developed a flourishing culture of science and literature, but this was the exception.

Intense anti-Judaism in Europe was the norm. The Crusaders, for example, on their way to liberate the Holy Land from the Muslims, attacked Jewish communities en route in areas such as the German Rhineland. Rumours about Jewish ritual murder were widespread, including the blood libel accusation that each Holy Week Jews killed a Christian, usually a child, as a sacrificial offering for Passover. By the end of the thirteenth century the mass murder of Jews had become a common occurrence in Germany and France. In England Jews were murdered while trying to give gifts to the King at Richard I's coronation and 150 Jews were massacred in York in 1190. A century later they were all expelled from England and shortly afterwards from France. In the fifteenth century Jews were persecuted during the Spanish Inquisition and in 1492 expelled from Spain. In the 1520s in Germany, Martin Luther initially expressed sympathy for Jewish suffering, but once he realized they would not convert to his branch of Christianity, he preached viciously against them towards the end of his life.

Classical anti-Judaism began to decline in the late nineteenth century, and its formal end was symbolized by the Second Vatican Council (1962–5), which stated that Jews were to be regarded as still in covenant with God after Christ, that they could not be held collectively responsible for the death of Christ, and that Jesus and the early Church were profoundly influenced by the Jewish teachings of their time. Anti-Judaism still exists today, notably in the Orthodox Church, which includes the description of Jews as 'deiciders' in the Eastern Liturgy, but it is rare in the Roman Catholic and Protestant churches.

The coming of the modern era, and a measure of social liberation, did result in political freedom for individual Jews in certain countries, but not for the Jewish people as a community. It also led to a revival of anti-Semitism. In Russia, the situation was particularly difficult and Jewish communities faced frequent pogroms and attacks.

THE DREYFUS AFFAIR

The Dreyfus Affair, 1894, illustrated the anti-Semitic environment of late nineteenth-century Europe. A French army captain and Jew, Alfred Dreyfus, was tried for treason, found guilty and court-martialled by anti-Semitic army officers on the basis of forged documents, then sent to life imprisonment on Devil's Island off the coast of French Guyana. The Dreyfus Affair caused civil unrest in France and in 1898 was the subject of a front-page, open letter in the press from the novelist Émile Zola to the French president, headlined 'J'accuse . . .!' To the French nationalistic and religious right, Dreyfus the Jew symbolized all the liberal, alien and de-Christianizing pressures on the traditional Christian order in the country. The publication of 'J'accuse . . .!' was followed by anti-Semitic riots in France. Synagogues were attacked and Zola had to flee to England. Dreyfus underwent a second trial in 1899. The military judges again found him guilty but 'with extenuating circumstances', sentencing him to ten years' imprisonment. A few months later he was granted a pardon. Nearly a hundred years later, in 1995, the French army officially declared Dreyfus innocent.

The Church viewed Jews as a threat to the Christian culture of Europe and propounded a 'teaching of contempt'. It was this that sowed the seeds of hatred and made it so easy for Hitler to use anti-Semitism as a political weapon. With some noble exceptions, the Church was silent during the horrors of 1933–45. Although no one would deny that Nazism was opposed to Christianity, Hitler justified anti-Semitism with reference to Christian attitudes towards Judaism and found much in

Christian teaching that the Nazis could use. During this period, six million Jews perished alongside five million non-Jews (including gypsies, Serbs, members of the Polish intelligentsia, resistance fighters from all the nations, German opponents of Nazism, homosexuals, Jehovah's Witnesses, habitual criminals, and those considered generally 'anti-social', like beggars, vagrants and hawkers). The Holocaust was a carefully planned act of mass murder.

Major Concentration and Death Camps

www.jewishvirtuallibrary.org/jsource/Holocaust/ccmap1.html

NUMBERS OF JEWS MURDERED IN THE HOLOCAUST BY COUNTRY

Austria 50,000 –27% (of Jewish population)
Lithuania 143,000 – 85.1%
Netherlands 100,000 – 71.4%
Poland 3,000,000 – 90.9%
Romania 287,000 – 47.1%
Germany 141,500 – 25%
Greece 67,000 – 86.6%
France 75,000 – 25%
Soviet Union 1,100,000 – 36.4%
Hungary 569,000 – 69%
Yugoslavia 63,300 – 81.2%

(*Source*: Encyclopaedia of the Holocaust;
http://motlc.wiesenthal.com/resources/questions/#5

At the end of the war one third of the world's Jewish population had been murdered in the Holocaust.

Some Jews do not like to use the term 'Holocaust' because etymologically it has sacrificial overtones, meaning a 'burnt offering' to appease God. The word *Shoah* is used more often. It has connotations of destruction, rupture and doubt.

The Shoah shattered any liberal optimism of the opening of the twentieth century. (It also stimulated some bitter jokes such as the remark that when Hitler rose to power there were two types of Jews in Germany; pessimists and optimists. The pessimists fled into exile and the optimists went to the gas chambers.)

Not only the churches, but the academic institutions of Europe, the judiciary, industry, business, trade unions, teachers, the medical profession and journalists all betrayed the values of civilization in their failure to oppose the Nazis. For me, the Holocaust epitomizes the inadequacy of secular human values. Yet I am aware that the Holocaust also demonstrates the failure of religion. It is a profound challenge to all religious people and there are no easy answers that can evade the terror of the Shoah.

Rabbi Hugo Gryn once commented that the real question was not 'Where was God at Auschwitz?' but rather 'Where was man?' This rings true for many. For myself, the Shoah has led to an ongoing movement between doubt and faith, one which continues to hold me in tension.

Zionism and the Creation of the State of Israel

For many years, three Jewish friends meet daily in Tel Aviv for coffee. Over the years, they become more and more pessimistic about the situation in Israel, noticing the increase in terrorism, poor economic performance and a reduction in the number of tourists. One day, one of them announces that he has converted. 'What?' the other two exclaim. 'Yes,' he says. 'I've converted from being a pessimist to an optimist.' A few minutes later one of the pessimists turns to the newly converted optimist and says to him, 'If you have become an optimist, why do you still look so worried?' 'Ah,' his friend replies, 'do you think it's easy being an optimist?'

Jews have always had an attachment to and a presence in the Land of Israel. Even after the destruction of the Second Temple by the Romans and the expulsion of the Jews from Jerusalem, Jews looked forward to a messianic return in due course. There seems to have been a continuous if somewhat tenuous Jewish existence in the Holy Land. In the fourth century the Church

Father Jerome, who lived near Bethlehem, reported that there were few Christians and that most of the people in the country were Jews; in the fifth and sixth centuries there were flourishing rabbinical schools in Galilee and especially in the city of Tiberias. In the medieval period Jewish communities were regularly established in cities such as Acre and Safed.

In the second half of the nineteenth century a new type of immigrant to the Holy Land began to arrive, fleeing persecution in Russia and Eastern Europe. Collective agricultural settlements, known as *kibbutzim*, began in earnest. The arrival of significant numbers of Jews in the 1880s marked the beginning of modern Zionism, which led eventually to the creation of the modern State of Israel in 1948.

Theodore Herzl is known as the founder of the Jewish State. Attending the trial of Albert Dreyfus (Herzl was a journalist reporting for a Viennese newspaper), he argued that Jews could only be safe if they had their own land, and that Diaspora life would lead to catastrophe (borne out, tragically, by the Holocaust). He pictured the future Jewish state as a socialist utopia.

In 1917, the British Government issued the Balfour Declaration, agreeing that a Jewish state should be established in the Palestine region which they governed as a Protectorate. Over the next few years Jewish immigration increased and important institutions were founded, such as the Hebrew University in Jerusalem in 1925. Hebrew was reborn, recreated from a language of history and religion into a language of everyday life.

There had been strong and paramilitary opposition to British colonial rule for many years, and in 1947 the United Nations agreed to partition the contested land between Jews and Arabs. In May 1948 the British Government withdrew their forces and David Ben-Gurion became the first prime minister of the State of Israel. Immediately, the surrounding Arab states invaded and the new state was forced to fight the first of several major wars.

Many Arabs in Israel fled. Some expected the destruction of the Jewish state and planned to return a few weeks later. Others were simply fearful for their lives. Although some land was captured – Jordan annexed what has now become known as the West Bank in 1948 – Israel survived. But this War of Independence also marked the beginning of a Palestinian refugee crisis; many Palestinians were placed in refugee camps, refused citizenship in Arab countries and not allowed to return to Israel. They became pawns in a political game and suffered – and continue to suffer – greatly, while the conflict between Israel and her neighbours failed to be resolved.

For most of its history Israel has had a deeply troubled relationship with the Arab states that surround it. Notable among recent conflicts were the Six Day War in 1967, the Yom Kippur War in 1973–4 and the Lebanon War, which began in 1982 and ended officially when Israel removed all its troops from Lebanese soil in 2000. The first steps towards a permanent peace came when Israel signed a treaty with Egypt in 1979, and with Jordan in 1994. There have also been direct negotiations with the Palestinians, which have so far promised more than they have delivered. For Jews, the re-creation of a Jewish State in the Land of Israel nearly 2,000 years after the previous Jewish commonwealth is something of a miracle. It is somewhat miraculous that Israel survived its early years, sustained by the help and support of foreign allies such as Russia in the 1950s and more recently, the USA from the 1970s onwards.

Israel today cannot be understood simply by reference to biblical texts or rabbinic theology. Nor is its philosophy any longer dependent upon the writings of Herzl. Most Israelis do not live on a kibbutz. Although there was massive immigration to Israel from Russia in the 1990s, over half of Israel's Jews are of Middle Eastern or North African origin. In other words, there is no single, monolithic Israeli culture. Israelis – like Jews everywhere – are deeply divided. The creation of the State of Israel has brought renewed confidence to Jews both inside the Jewish state and also in the Diaspora, and also new problems and challenges.

Of the population of Israel 16% are Muslim Arabs (1.1 million) and 2% are Christian Arabs (140,000), who are full citizens of the Jewish state. Although the Israeli Arab population has its own press, school system, and members of parliament, there are striking imbalances between Jews and Arabs, for example in terms of resource allocation. These remain to be redressed. In the West Bank there are more than one million Palestinians, some of whom are under the governance of the Palestinian Authority. Most Israelis and Palestinians seek peaceful relations but this seems as far off as ever.

> A story is told about an Israeli and a Palestinian leader meeting with God and asking whether there will ever be peace in the Middle East. 'Of course there will be peace,' God tells them. They looked relieved. 'But,' God continues, 'not in my life-time.'

The territorial distances between the Palestinians and Israelis are smaller than the emotional gap between the two peoples. They do not trust each other. Israelis are angry with the Palestinians because they rejected the Camp David proposals in 2000 and returned to the use of terror. Palestinians are angry with the

Israelis because they live in poverty, under the constant threat of violence.

One hundred and twenty years after the beginning of modern Zionism, a peaceful solution still seems some distance away yet in their hearts both Israelis and Palestinians know that good neighbours are better than good guns.

4

What do Jews believe?

David Ben-Gurion once asked Martin Buber, 'Why, really, why do you believe in God?' Buber answered, 'If there were a God about which one can talk, I too would not believe. But since there is a God to which one can talk, I believe in Him'.

Monotheism

Judaism begins with the affirmation of one God. 'Hear, O Israel, the Lord is our God, the Lord is One' (Deuteronomy 6:4), which is the first line of the most famous Jewish prayer, the *Shema*. The prayer begins with recognition of God's oneness and uniqueness and moves on to the obligations which arise from this new knowledge: 'And you shall love the Lord your God with all your heart, with all your soul and all your might. And these words which I command you this day shall be upon your heart . . . and you shall teach them to your children.' (Deuteronomy 6:5–6)

Jews experience revelation in their biblical encounter with God. The Bible does not ask whether God exists but rather, what does God say to me? Why did God create me? What is my function in the world? The Bible portrays an encounter with a God who cares passionately and who addresses humanity in the quiet moments of its existence – the personal God of the Bible.

Britain's Chief Rabbi, Jonathan Sacks, once said that when he puts down a volume of Homer, he is no longer part of its world, but when he puts down the Hebrew Bible, he still hears the voice of God calling, 'Where are you?' The God of the Bible, he suggests, is not distant in time or detached but passionately engaged and present.

There is, however, an alternative stream of tradition exemplified by the medieval commentator Maimonides and followed by other Jewish philosophers, which rejects the idea of a personal God. Maimonides wrote numerous works, such as *The Guide for the Perplexed* and *Thirteen Principles of Faith,* which attempt to harmonize Aristotelian philosophy with the Bible. He believed there could be no contradiction between the truths God has revealed and the findings of the human mind. Maimonides was a follower of negative theology; that is, God can only be described by negative attributes. One cannot say, for example, that God exists; all one can say is that God is not non-existent. In this way, Maimonides (and later Christian scholastics whom he influenced) believed that the attempt to gain knowledge of God could only be achieved by describing what God is not, rather than what God is. This led him to the dictum, 'Teach your tongue to say "I do not know" and you will progress.'

However, for many Jews, myself included, the encounter with God is more than an acceptance of an intellectual proposition. I believe God cares about humanity and I believe in a personal God. When the seventeenth-century scientist and philosopher Blaise Pascal died, a note was discovered sewn into his overcoat. It read, 'Not the God of the Philosophers but the God of Abraham, Isaac and Jacob.' Pascal had come to realize that although 'proofs' of God's existence can be approached rationally and by philosophical means, it is only the exceptional mind which follows an intellectual pathway to an encounter with the Divine. More often than not, it is personal encounter which is decisive.

Most Jews do not follow the philosophical tradition set out by Maimonides. It is a far more common Jewish principle that although God can be experienced, God cannot be understood because God is utterly unlike humankind. All statements in the Bible and in rabbinic literature, which use anthropomorphism, for example, are understood as linguistic metaphors, otherwise it would be impossible to talk about God at all. This is demonstrated by the question Moses asked when he first encountered God:

> 'When they [the Children of Israel] say to me: what is His name? What shall I say to them?' And God said to Moses: Eh'yeh asher eh'yeh – I AM THAT I AM; and He said, 'This you shall say to the Children of Israel: I AM has sent me to you. (Exodus 3:14)

God's reply is understood on one level as 'He for whom no word or name is sufficient', but Buber taught that it means 'I am where I shall be encountered', for God who is truly God cannot be expressed but only addressed. Buber developed this further in his book *I and Thou*. He maintained that a personal relationship with God is only truly personal when there is not only awe and respect on the human side but when we are not overcome or overwhelmed in our relationship with God.

Torah

Although Judaism affirms monotheism first and foremost, it has never developed any one binding catechism. Rabbis such as Maimonides did propose a number of basic principles of faith that one is expected to uphold, but there are disputes over the precise number of formulations of beliefs. Joseph Albo, a fifteenth-century Spanish rabbi and theologian, for instance, counts three, while Maimonides lists thirteen. The difference and the alternative lists provided by other rabbinic authorities indicate a broad level of tolerance for variant views.

The rabbis did, however, agree on the centrality and individuality of the Torah, a word derived from the Hebrew verb 'to teach', which refers to the books of the Pentateuch: Genesis, Exodus, Leviticus, Numbers and Deuteronomy. Rabbinic Judaism holds that the Torah read today is the same as that given to Moses by God on Mount Sinai.

Alongside the five books, known as the Written Torah (or sometimes as *Chumash*, derived from the Hebrew word for 'five') is the Oral Torah, which is an ongoing exposition of the Written Torah. Thus, the whole Torah embodies Jewish teachings from the revelation at Sinai to the modern day.

An oral tradition was needed to accompany the written one because the Written Torah alone, even with its 613 commandments, is an insufficient guide to Jewish life. For example, the fourth of the Ten Commandments, states, 'Remember the Sabbath day and keep it holy' (Exodus 20:8). From the Sabbath's inclusion in the Ten Commandments, it is clearly regarded as important. Yet, when one looks for the specific biblical laws regulating how to observe the day, one finds only injunctions against lighting a fire, leaving one's home, cutting down a tree, ploughing and harvesting. Would merely refraining from these few activities fulfil the biblical command to make the Sabbath holy? Indeed, the rituals that are most commonly associated with the Sabbath – lighting candles, blessing bread and wine, and the weekly reading of the Torah – are found not in the Written but, rather, in the Oral Torah.

Another example from the oral tradition is demonstrated by the need to mitigate certain laws that would have caused grave problems if carried out literally, such as 'an eye for an eye, a tooth for a tooth' (Exodus 21:24). A literal reading would indicate that if one person blinded another, he should be blinded in return. However, the Oral Torah understands the verse in terms of monetary compensation: the value of an eye, the value of a tooth.

Ultra-Orthodox Jews believe that the Torah today is no different from what was received by Moses from God. Orthodox Jews are divided, some suggesting that over time a few scribal errors may have crept into the text. They note that the Masoretes, scribes of the seventh to tenth centuries, compared all known Torah variations in order to create a definitive text, but for all practical purposes Orthodox Jews view the Written and Oral Torah as identical to that which Moses taught.

This does not imply that the text of the Torah should be understood literally, for God conveyed not only the words of the Torah, but also its meaning. God gave rules as to how the laws were to be understood and implemented, and these were passed down as an oral tradition. This was eventually written in the Mishnah and the Talmud.

Progressive Jews – a term that includes Liberal, Reform, Conservative and other non-orthodox religious groups – generally accept that, while divinely revealed, the Torah was written down by human hand and therefore contains error as well as truth. Accepting the findings of biblical scholarship, archaeo-logical and linguistic research, most Progressive Jews accept that the core of the Written Torah comes from Moses, but maintain that the Torah read today has been edited together from several documents.

Progressive Jews emphasize continuous revelation, that is, the prophecy of Moses was the first in a long chain of revelation in which mankind gradually began to understand the will of God better and better. As such, they maintain that the laws of Moses are no longer binding in their literal interpretation, and it is today's generation that must assess what God wants of them.

An example of the difference in approach can be seen in the statement in Genesis that God created the world in six days. While most ultra-Orthodox Jews take this literally, many Modern Orthodox and Progressive Jews feel that the six days should be interpreted as stages in the creation of the universe and the earth. Another significant difference is that for Progressive Jews, an emphasis on personal autonomy overrides traditional Jewish law and custom; the individual decides which Jewish practices to adopt as binding.

For their part, secular and humanist Jews, while rejecting any divine aspect, still view the Torah as central to maintaining the Jewishness of life. Although their focus is on Judaism as a culture rather than a religion, they value the Torah for what it teaches in order to live an ethical Jewish life. Secular Jews are often criticized by religious Jews for their rather tenuous 'bagel connection' with Judaism (and it is unclear whether secular Judaism is suitably robust and self-sufficient to be successfully transmitted to future generations). It is noteworthy that the Torah, and Jewish observance, remain central to Jewish practice, whatever the depth of belief.

Covenant

> One day a Jewish mother and her eight-year-old daughter were
> walking along a beach. Suddenly, a gigantic wave hit the shore,
> sweeping the little girl out to sea. 'Oh, God,' lamented the
> mother, turning her face towards heaven and shaking her fist.
> 'This is my only child. She is the love and joy of my life. I have
> cherished every day that she has been with me. Give her back to
> me and I will go to the synagogue every day for the rest of my
> life!'
>
> Suddenly, another gigantic wave hit the beach but this time
> deposited the girl back on the sand. The mother looked up to
> heaven and said, 'She had a hat on!'

The tradition of arguing with God has a long history, going
back to biblical times. Abraham, for example, famously argued
with God when the cities of Sodom and Gomorrah were about
to be destroyed. The willingness to enter into a personal con-
versation, captured in Isaiah's comment (Isaiah 1:12), 'Come
now let us reason together', demonstrates the close relationship between the Jewish people and God. For Jews, the Bible is
not simply what happened in the distant past to someone else:
it is personal memory, my story, what happened to my ancestors
and therefore, in so far as I carry on their story, to me. The
Torah speaks not of moral truths in the abstract but of commands, which is to say, truths addressed to me, calling for my
response.

God initiates a covenant with a community – the Jewish
people – and that community accepts certain obligations and
responsibilities as His partner. The English word 'covenant' is
the standard translation of the Hebrew '*b'rit*', generally understood as agreement. B'rit was translated into Greek as 'decree'

(*diathèkè*) and into Latin as 'testament' (*testamentum*), which became the Christian designation of both parts of the Christian Bible – the Old and the New Testaments.

For Jews, the Bible describes how the Children of Israel entered into a relationship with God through God's election. 'You are the children of the Lord your God . . . You are a holy people to the Lord your God and the Lord has chosen you out of all the peoples on earth to be a people for His own possession (*segulah*).' (Deuteronomy 14:1–2) The word segulah refers to a special possession, implying that although all peoples belong to the Lord, Israel is particularly cherished and its people are to become known as a holy people. Understanding this covenant is key to understanding what Jews believe.

In biblical times the covenant was regularly renewed, initially with the patriarchs and later with the whole people of Israel at Sinai, in a ceremony in which they finally accepted the obligations of the Torah. The covenant was renewed again by Ezra after the destruction of the First Temple in 587 BCE, and by the prophets, who regularly berated Israel for breaking its side of the agreement. God's fidelity to Israel, in spite of their stubbornness and misdemeanours, is a common biblical theme, as witnessed by the story of the Golden Calf, which describes how the Israelites used jewellery to make a calf while Moses was receiving the Ten Commandments on Mount Sinai. Although they explicitly disobeyed God and worshipped the idol, God showed compassion and decided not to 'blot out' the Israelites for their actions. The covenant with God and God's compassion for Israel are further developed in the rabbinic writings and in Jewish liturgy. The new covenant mentioned by prophets such as Jeremiah, which Christians view as looking forwards to Jesus, is understood by Jews as a call for spiritual renewal and revival rather than a new covenant replacing the old.

God's covenant with Israel is associated especially with the Land of Israel. In Genesis 17:8 God states: 'I will give to you and to your descendants after you the land of your sojournings, all the land of Canaan for an everlasting possession; and I will be their God.' The Promised Land is understood by Jews as an integral part of the covenant.

Another aspect of covenant is that Israel is not chosen out of arbitrary preference for a particular people but in order that God's name be blessed. God and the people of God are described as partners. A two-way relationship is emphasized. The Jewish people are expected to respond to God by being faithful to the Torah and by keeping the covenant. Thus, the covenant assumes mutuality, for the two parties – divine and human – make an agreement.

The Jewish understanding of covenant, based on the experience of Sinai, implies that the conditions of the divine partner have already been met. Consequently, it has always been assumed that the covenant brings responsibility for the people of God to fulfil their obligations . . . But what happens should God fail to fulfil His part of the covenant? A fundamental challenge to the covenant between God and Israel occurred during the years 1933–45. The horrors of the Holocaust have, for many Jews, shaken to the core their relationship with God.

Responses to the Holocaust

Elie Wiesel, a well-known Holocaust survivor, recounts how three great Jewish scholars created a rabbinic court of law in Auschwitz. Their purpose was to indict God. The trial lasted several nights. Witnesses were heard, evidence was gathered, conclusions were drawn, all of which finally issued in a unanimous verdict: the Lord God Almighty, Creator of Heaven and

Earth, was found guilty of crimes against humanity and of breaking His covenant with the Children of Israel. What happened next was astonishing. After what Wiesel described as an 'infinity of silence', one of the Talmudic scholars looked at the sky and said, 'It's time for evening prayers', and the members of the tribunal proceeded to recite Ma-ariv, the evening service.

The question 'Where was God in Auschwitz?' remains a theological challenge for all people, and especially Jews. Many are convinced that, after the Shoah, theology can never be the same again.

There are many religious responses to the Holocaust. Some ultra-Orthodox Jews speak of the Shoah as a punishment for Israel's unfaithfulness. Others link the horrors with the miracle of the rebirth of the State of Israel. Still others find their faith in God shattered and believe that God quite simply deserted his people. Some thinkers have spoken of a limited God who is not in total control; others have spoken of a God who suffers or who shares human suffering.

Many, like me, find themselves swinging between doubt and faith.

Another well-known Holocaust survivor was the London rabbi, Hugo Gryn. 'I believe that God was there Himself,' he said, 'violated and blasphemed.' He tells how on the Day of Atonement, he fasted and hid amongst the stacks of insulation boards. He tried to remember the prayers that he had learned as a child at synagogue and asked God for forgiveness. Eventually, he says, 'I dissolved in crying. I must have sobbed for hours . . . Then, I seemed to be granted a curious inner peace . . . I believe God was also crying . . . I found God.' But it was not the God of his childhood, the God whom he had expected miraculously to rescue the Jewish people.

Hugo Gryn found God in the camps, but God was crying. Other thinkers have also spoken of a suffering God. Martin Buber adopted the phrase, 'eclipse of God', and suggested that each generation of Jews need to 'struggle' with the Holocaust in their attempt to come to terms with it. The name Israel was particularly apt because it means, 'he who struggles with God'. After the Shoah, Buber asked, 'Dare we recommend to the survivors of Auschwitz, to the Job of the gas chambers, "Thank ye the Lord for He is good, for His mercy endures for ever"?' (Psalm 111:1)

Elie Wiesel could not speak or write about his experiences during the Holocaust for a decade. Until the early 1960s, silence seemed to be a universal response. Many survivors found that the post-war societies in which they lived were not open to listening to their stories. Most were occupied with rebuilding their own lives rather than dwelling on others' experiences. Only later, did survivors begin to recall their lives during the Holocaust.

Richard Rubenstein, an American Jewish thinker, concluded that it was not possible to believe in divine election and providence because this was an absurd interpretation of Jewish history. He claimed that traditional belief in God was dead and that, instead, Jews had to reinterpret their heritage and become a 'normal' nation. Rubenstein aimed to demythologize Judaism, yet keep the traditions and observances, which helped maintain its distinctive identity. Within this new interpretative framework, the State of Israel became central, since it established a political normality, taken for granted by other nations whose states had existed for much longer.

Emil Fackenheim, a Canadian Jewish philosopher, rejected the claim that God was dead, and defined the Holocaust as a unique event that held significance not only for Jews, but also for all humanity. What happened might be explained, he suggested, but *why* the Holocaust occurred was impossible to understand. Yet, while the Holocaust is without meaning, it issues a commandment, the 614th. He wrote that 'the authentic Jew of today is forbidden to hand Hitler yet another posthumous victory'. To this end Jews must retain their identity, resist assimilation and only marry within their faith. In addition, he calls for the tension between 'religious' and 'secular' Jews to be resolved.

Fackenheim also introduced the notion of *tikkun olam* ('mending the world'), a mystical concept to describe the human effort of relating to God. The better the relationship between Jews and God, the more 'whole' the world becomes and the less fractured the relationship between God and humanity. After the Holocaust, such mending is more difficult and, Fackenheim claims, all the more necessary.

American Jewish theologian Irving Greenberg has also grappled theologically with the Holocaust. He suggests that the Holocaust represents the beginning of a third era of the covenant between God and Israel. In the biblical age, the Exodus represented redemption; in the rabbinic age, the destruction of the Temple represented tragedy. In the modern age, while the Holocaust represents destruction the rebirth of the State of Israel represents redemption.

Greenberg concluded that the Holocaust requires a radical rethinking of the conditions under which the Jewish people commit themselves to the covenant. In the Holocaust, the covenant was endangered because of the potential death of the whole Jewish people. However, Jews have responded with a continuing commitment to remain Jewish, which, Greenberg suggests, represents a new stage: the voluntary covenant.

The voluntary covenant acknowledges the rupture of the Holocaust but also affirms that the relationship has not ended. For Greenberg, the relationship between God and the Jewish people has been renewed, this time at the initiative of the people. The Jewish people no longer owe obedience to God (for they were not in the wrong) but voluntarily act out of renewed hope.

Judaism as a way of life: *Shabbat* and the festivals

> On the seventh day God finished the work, which He had been doing, and He ceased on the seventh day from all the work, which He had done.
>
> (Genesis 2:2)

Rashi, a famous tenth-century French rabbi, asked how it was possible for God to finish the work of creation on the seventh day if at the same time He ceased from all work on the seventh day? Rashi explained that creation could only be completed by a day of rest.

At the end of the first chapter of Genesis, God surveys all that had been created over the first six days and finds it 'very good'. At the beginning of chapter two, God ceases (*shavat*) creating and blesses the seventh day to make it holy. The Sabbath (from the Hebrew root meaning 'to cease') is a weekly day of rest observed from sunset on Friday night until nightfall the following evening.

Judaism accords the Sabbath the status of a holy day for it is the first holy day mentioned in the Bible and God was the first to observe it. As well as commemorating God's creation of the universe, Shabbat represents a taste of a future messianic world. In fact, there is a traditional belief that the messiah will come if every Jew properly observes two consecutive Sabbaths.

The Bible describes how work was banned on the Sabbath for all, including slaves and animals. 'Six days shall you work but on the seventh day there shall be to you a holy day, a

Sabbath of solemn rest to the Lord.' (Exodus 35:2) Later, the rabbis developed thirty-nine categories of work, which were forbidden. For many Jews, the Sabbath is primarily a day of rest but, as the following Chassidic story makes clear, physical rest or respite from work is not an end in itself:

A man left his home and went to work in a far-off place. Whenever a stranger visited he would ask whether they knew his family but no one had news. After many months he met a beggar, and asked him many questions. The beggar told him that he had no time to answer since he had to beg for alms. 'Tell me,' the anxious man inquired, 'how much money do you collect each day?' 'Three to four pieces of gold,' replied the beggar. 'Look, I'll give you four pieces of gold, but in return, stay with me all day and tell me what you know about my family.'

The beggar agreed to meet the man the day before he returned home. The day arrived but hardly had the man begun to talk when the beggar fell asleep. When he woke up he said he felt too weak to answer questions and needed a meal. His request was granted and he ate and drank while his host left him undisturbed. At last, he had eaten his fill but instead of continuing his account he said that he had eaten too much and needed a rest. The patience of the employer was at an end and he angrily said, 'I have engaged your services for the whole day and all you have done is eat, drink, and sleep until you've practically wasted the entire day which should have been devoted to me . . .'

The story is a reminder to Jews that the Sabbath should be a time for prayer, both at home and in synagogue and not simply a day of rest. In synagogue, the reading of the Torah is the central part of the Saturday morning service. According to Jewish mystical writings, the Sabbath represents both the male and female principles in the Godhead, which are united on this day like no other. Perhaps this is one reason why marital intercourse is regarded as especially meritorious on Friday night.

Some of the best-known Sabbath customs surround the Friday night meal, which begins with a blessing over two candles, followed by a prayer over wine and over the bread, called *challa*, which consists of two loaves. These serve as a reminder of the two portions of manna gathered by the Israelites in the desert on the Sabbath eve.

For Jews, the Sabbath ends with Saturday evening prayers, called *havdalah*, ('separation'), to mark the transition from the holy day to the secular week.

The autumn festivals

The busiest time of year in the Jewish calendar is the autumn, when four festivals take place within a month. The season begins with the Jewish New Year, *Rosh Hashana*, held on the first and second of the Hebrew month of *Tishri*, which has but one similarity with the celebrations that surround the end of the secular New Year, on 31 December – the making of New Year resolutions. Rosh Hashana is a time not of parties but of looking back at the mistakes of the year just ended and reflecting on the changes in lifestyle that are needed to lead a better life in the year ahead.

This reflection includes seeking reconciliation with people who have been wronged during the year. The rabbis explain that before asking God for forgiveness of sins, we must first seek to right the wrongs we have committed against others. Consequently, Rosh Hashana is a solemn festival, requiring self-reflection. It also marks the beginning of a ten-day period, which ends with the observance of *Yom Kippur*, the Day of Atonement. The Ten Days of Awe, as they are sometimes called, are a time for *Teshuva* (repentance), *Tefilla* (prayer) and *Tzedaka* (charity).

During the Rosh Hashana service, which lasts between three and four hours, the community hears the primitive sounds of a ram's horn (called a *shofar*) being blown on over a hundred occasions. According to Maimonides its purpose is to wake up the congregation and to prompt Jews to think about what they can do to make themselves better people.

A rabbi and a student were going to synagogue on the eve of Rosh Hashana when a sudden downpour forced them to seek shelter at the door of a tavern. The student peered through one of the windows and saw a group of Jews feasting, drinking and partying. He told the rabbi that these men were behaving badly when they should have been in synagogue praying for God's forgiveness for their sins. Disregarding the student's rebuke the rabbi said, 'They are surely reciting the benedictions for food and drink. May God bless these men.' The student continued to eavesdrop. 'Woe to us, rabbi!' he exclaimed. 'I have just heard two of them telling each other of the thefts they committed.' 'If that be so,' said the rabbi, 'they are truly observant Jews. They are confessing their sins before Rosh Hashana. As you know, no one is more righteous than he who repents.'

Yom Kippur, the Day of Atonement, occurs on the tenth Tishri, and is the holiest day of the year. According to Leviticus 23:26, Yom Kippur is set aside to 'afflict the soul' to atone for the sins of the past year. Traditionally all Jewish adults, defined as those over the age of thirteen, fast and pray. Often Jews, who do not observe any other custom, will fast or acknowledge the seriousness of this day one way or another. Some friends of mine who are not at all observant (even those who are devout atheists) attend synagogue. They particularly enjoy the traditional music and feel a sense of connection with other Jews who are observing the day.

Observant Jews spend most if not all the day in synagogue.

Services begin early in the morning, often around 9 a.m. and continue until evening, ending with a long blast of the shofar.

There are many additions to the regular synagogue prayers, the most important being the *Al Chet,* or *Vidui,* the confession of sins. All sins are confessed in the plural ('we are guilty', etc), emphasizing communal responsibility, of which we are all part. Another feature of the Yom Kippur service is the reading of the Book of Jonah to teach that if people are sincere in their prayers God will always accept their Teshuva, even from an entire city of sinners.

According to Ecclesiastes 7:20, 'There is not a righteous man upon earth that does good and sins not.' Sin separates humanity from God but repentance provides a way back, for God will show compassion. The Bible has many words for regret or repent, but the most common is *shuv,* ('to turn, return'), which is the basis for the word Teshuvah. Thus, repentance means turning back to God, turning from the ways of evil to the ways of right-eousness. As the prophet Malachi put it, '"Return unto Me and I will return unto you" says the Lord of Hosts.' (Malachi 3:7)

The story is told that a rabbi once asked an illiterate tailor what he did on Yom Kippur, given that he could not read the prescribed prayers. The tailor reluctantly replied, 'I spoke to God and told Him that the sins for which I am expected to repent are minor ones. I also said to Him, "My sins are incon-sequential; I may have kept some leftover cloth or occasionally forgotten to recite some prayers. But you have committed some really grave sins. You removed mothers from their children and children from their mothers. So let's reach an agreement. If You'll pardon me, I'm ready to pardon You."'

The rabbi angrily rebuked the illiterate Jew. 'You were too lenient with God. You should have insisted that He bring redemption to the world.'

SUKKOT AND SIMCHAT TORAH

The third major autumn festival is *Sukkot*, which means
'booths'. A *sukkah* is built of branches and leaves with
openings to enable the light of the sun, moon and stars to
be seen. In celebration of the harvest, the sukkah is
decorated with fruits and vegetables hung from the roof
and the walls. The Talmud commends Jews to 'dwell in the
Sukkah as you would live in your home'. However, even
most Orthodox Jews fulfil the *mitzvah* by simply eating
meals and studying in the sukkah.

In biblical times Sukkot was solely a harvest festival but
later it took on additional meaning, recalling the temporary
shelters in which the Children of Israel lived while they
wandered through the desert for forty years.

On the last day of Sukkot Jews celebrate *Simchat Torah*,
'Rejoicing in the Torah', which marks the completion of the
annual cycle of weekly Torah readings. During the year,
Jews read a portion of the Torah each week and on
Simchat Torah Jews read the last verses of Deuteronomy
and the first verses of Genesis, demonstrating that the
Torah is a circle which never ends.

Although Simchat Torah is not mentioned in the Bible or
in the Talmud (it became a festival by the eleventh century
CE), the completion of the readings is a time of great
celebration. According to tradition, Simchat Torah is one of
the two times of the year when Jews are commanded to
drink heavily! There are processions, *Hakafot*, around the
synagogue carrying Torah scrolls and plenty of high-spirited
singing and dancing.

The winter festivals: *Chanukah* and *Tu-bishvat*

Chanukah, known as the Festival of Lights, is observed for eight days in winter and commemorates the military victory of the Maccabees over the Syrian Greeks who ruled Israel around 2,200 years ago. Chanukah means 'dedication' and refers to the rededication of the Temple in Jerusalem in 165 BCE. The Festival of Lights refers to the flames kindled on each night on the *Hanukkiya*, a nine-branch candelabra (see image on front cover). On each night one more candle is added and lit, beginning with one on the first night of Chanukah and ending with the eighth on the final evening. The ninth branch is reserved for the *shamash*, the servant light, which is lit first and used to kindle the other lights.

Chanukah is popular with children, particularly among communities living in Christian countries. Some scholars suggest that Chanukah increased in importance in these countries because it represented a Jewish response to the Christian celebrations of the birth of Christ on 25 December. Not only does Chanukah take place around the same time as Christmas (is it coincidental that it begins on the twenty-fifth day of the Jewish month of *Kislev*?), but there are also a number of similar customs such as the lighting of candles and the giving of presents. It is ironic that this holiday, which has its roots in a revolution against the assimilation and suppression of Judaism, has become the most assimilated, secular holiday on the Jewish calendar.

One month later, Jews celebrate *Tu-bishvat*, the New Year for Trees, which is an opportunity to reflect on human responsibility as 'stewards of the world'. It is traditional to eat fruits and plant trees. Scholars believe that in biblical times Tu-bishvat was an agricultural festival, but after the destruction of the Temple, Jews marked their attachment to the Land of Israel by eating foods that could be found there.

The Bible extols reverence for fruit trees as symbols of God's bounty and beneficence. Special laws were formulated to protect trees in times of war and to ensure that their produce would not be picked until they were mature enough. In modern times, Tu-bishvat has enjoyed a revival as a celebration of the environment as well as reminding Jews of their attachment to Israel. The medieval mystical *Tu-bishvat seder* has also been revived and transformed into a celebration of the environment.

The spring festivals: *Purim, Pesach* and *Shavuot*

Purim

Purim, which means 'lots', celebrates the story of Esther and takes place on the fourteenth day of the Jewish month of *Adar*, usually in March. Esther, along with her uncle, Mordecai, helped save the community of Persia from the murderous intentions of Haman, the wicked advisor to the king, who wanted to annihilate the Jewish people. The Book of Esther reads as a folk tale and is the only book of the Bible that does not contain the name of God.

The primary custom of Purim is to hear the reading of the book of Esther, known as the *Megillah*, which means scroll. Purim often ends up as a communal party since Jews by tradition are commanded to eat, drink and be merry. According to the Talmud, a person is required to drink until he cannot tell the difference between 'cursed be Haman' and 'blessed be Mordecai', though opinions differ as to exactly how drunk that is. It is also customary to boo, hiss, stamp feet and shake rattles whenever the name of Haman is mentioned in the service.

Pesach

Pesach, Passover, is a family-orientated festival when Jews re-tell the story, known as the *Haggadah* (Hebrew for 'to tell, relate') of the Exodus from Egypt and thank God for redeeming them 'with an outstretched arm'. It takes place on fifteenth day of the Jewish month of *Nisan*, and is called in the Bible *hag ha-Pesach* ('the festival of passing over') and *hag ha-Mazzot* ('festival of *matzah*').

The most well-known feature of the celebration of Passover today is the *seder* meal. The word 'seder' is derived from Aramaic, meaning 'order of service'. It is a feast, which takes place on the first two nights of Passover. The most important people at the seder are the children. The Haggadah states that in every generation, each person must feel as if he personally had come out of Egypt. 'You should tell your child on that day, "When I left Egypt the Lord did miracles for me . . .".'. Thus, parents are commanded to tell their children the story of the Israelite exodus from Egypt.

Other elements of the seder meal include:

- eating bitter herbs (because the Egyptians enslaved the Israelites and made their lives bitter)
- drinking four cups of wine (representing God's promises of redemption)
- eating unleavened bread (because the Israelites did not have time to ferment dough before they left Egypt)
- reclining to the left during parts of the service before the meal (symbolizing freedom, since Roman freemen reclined to the left)
- searching for the *afikomen* (a piece of matzah which is hidden during the seder and which children seek at the end of the meal)

During the meal, the Seder Plate is explained to all, and especially children, because it holds all of the main symbols of

Passover: a roasted shank bone, representing the Temple sacrifices in biblical times; a roasted egg, representing the offerings given in the Temple; parsley, reminding Jews that Passover corresponds with the spring harvest; a dish of chopped apples, nuts, and wine called *Charoset*, which represents the mortar used by the Israelites in bondage; finally, bitter herbs which represents the bitterness of slavery.

Shavuot

While Passover represents physical freedom from bondage and slavery, *Shavuot*, which commemorates the giving of the Torah to the Children of Israel on Mount Sinai, represents spiritual freedom from the bondage of idolatry. It is also called Feast of Weeks (shavuot means 'weeks') and stands for the seven weeks between Passover and Shavuot. The giving of the Torah is far more than a historical event and the rabbis compare it to a wedding between God and the Children of Israel. According to tradition, it was at this point that the Jews agreed to become God's Chosen People and the Lord became our God.

A well-established custom calls for all-night Torah study on the first night of Shavuot. There are many reasons given for the custom. My favourite is that when the Children of Israel were due to receive the Torah, they overslept. According to the Jewish mystical work, the Zohar, pious individuals therefore remain awake all night as an act of atonement. In some congregations, rabbis lecture deep into the night, either to enable the entire congregation to study the same topic or perhaps to accommodate those who are not capable of studying by themselves (or perhaps to put some congregants to sleep?).

During the Shavuot service, Jews listen to the reading of the Ten Commandments, which symbolize the giving of the whole Torah:

THE TEN COMMANDMENTS

I am the Lord, your God, who took you out from the land of Egypt, out of the camp of slavery.

You shall have no other gods but me.

You shall not take the name of the Lord, your God, in vain.

Remember the Sabbath day and keep it holy.

Honour your Father and your Mother.

You shall not murder.

You shall not commit adultery.

You shall not steal.

You shall not bear false witness against your neighbour.

You shall not covet your neighbour's house.

The new festivals: *Yom ha-Shoah* and *Yom ha-Atzmaut*

In the twentieth century, two new festivals have been added to the Jewish calendar – *Yom ha-Shoah*, Holocaust Remembrance Day, observed on the twenty-seventh Nisan, a few days after Pesach, and *Yom ha-Atzmaut*, Israel Independence Day, observed ten days later.

Yom ha-Shoah was first instituted by Israel's parliament, the

Knesset, in 1951 to mourn the six million Jews who perished in the Holocaust. It is now commemorated by Jews in the Diaspora as well. *Yom ha-Atzmaut* marks the establishment of the modern state of Israel, observed on the fifth *Iyar*, corresponding to 14 May 1948, the day Israel was declared an independent state.

The creation of two new festivals demonstrates the continuing vitality of Judaism and also illustrates that Judaism is a way of life. In this case, life – in the creation of the state of Israel – overcame death – in the devastation wreaked by the Holocaust. Indeed, some commentators suggest that the creation of the State of Israel represents the spiritual and physical resurrection of the Jewish people.

5

Varieties of belief

This chapter describes the lives of five Jews who demonstrate the diversity of the Jewish way of life today.

Woody Allen

> The important thing, I think, is not to be bitter . . . If it turns out that there is a God, I don't think that he is evil. I think that the worst thing you could say is that he is, basically, an under-achiever. If God exists, I hope he has a good excuse.

Woody Allen, born Allen Stewart Königsberg in 1935 in Brooklyn, New York, is an American film director and screen-writer who is one of the most widely respected and prolific film-makers of the modern era. Allen is the quintessential New York Jewish intellectual: neurotic and self-absorbed, cosmopolitan yet insecure, with a self-deprecating sense of humour.

As a child, he attended a Hebrew school and then a local elementary school where, due to his slight build, he later joked he 'was savagely beaten by children of all races and creeds'. He was soon noted for a talent at writing jokes. At the age of sixteen he started writing for television and changed his name to Woody Allen. He was expelled from New York University, which he later claimed was because he was caught 'cheating on my metaphysics final. You know, I looked within the soul of the boy sitting next to me.' A gifted comedian from an early stage, Allen won his first Emmy Award in 1957.

Allen turned his weaknesses into strengths and developed into an art form the neurotic, nervous, shy figure, which has become immortalized in films such as *Annie Hall* and *Manhattan*. For example, in the Oscar-winning film, *Radio Days*, Allen plays the narrator who is part of an extended Jewish family in 1940s New York. Everything about the family is Jewish, not just the social context, speech and mannerisms, but also the less definable aspects, such as a compulsion to dream, to aspire to a better life, to move one's family onwards, together with an abundance of sentimentality. The immigrant sensibilities which epitomize many of Allen's Jewish characters are alive with vitality, superstition and anxiety. Another common Jewish trait in the film is that they argue.

Woody Allen is intensely conscious of his Judaism and proud of it, unlike an earlier generation of Jewish comedy actors such as the Marx Brothers. They disguised their Jewishness. Groucho's moustache, Chico's Italian accent, Harpo's blond wig and their Italian names were ways of hiding their origins, whereas Woody Allen's characters reveal both inwardly and outwardly their Jewishness.

The change in American Jewish self-assurance in the Arts began in the late 1950s, just when Woody Allen was starting his career. Hollywood not only began to discover the Shoah but also to romanticize Israel, the *shtetl* of pre-Holocaust Eastern Europe and the Lower East Side of Manhattan. A new generation of actors appeared who looked and sounded Jewish: Dustin

Hoffman, Barbra Streisand and, more recently, Billy Crystal and Ben Stiller, actors with Brooklyn accents and Jewish gestures who often shrugged, complained and joked about any subject from life to death. In the words of Woody Allen:

> The chief problem about death, incidentally, is the fear that there may be no afterlife – a depressing thought, particularly for those who have bothered to shave. Also, there is the fear that there is an afterlife but no one will know where it's being held.

Hugo Gryn

> Hugo Gryn was fond of quoting Martin Luther King's remark that, 'We are caught in an inescapable network of mutuality. Whatever affects one directly affects all indirectly.' A story is told of a meeting between leaders of the Jewish and the Black communities in aid of establishing a Race and Community Group in Parliament. One person, on being asked, 'Why are Jewish people so interested in this work?', replied, 'Because it is right. Because it is needed. Because we want to be useful, in passing on just a little of the experience which we have gained, as earlier immigrants than you.' 'Wrong,' Hugo Gryn intervened. 'We are interested because this work is in our own interests. Our community can only flourish in a decent society which respects the rights of all minorities. So attacks on the Black community are a direct threat to us.'

Rabbi Hugo Gryn was born in the Carpathian town of Berehovo in Czechoslovakia in 1928, deported to Auschwitz at the age of thirteen and came to Britain with a group of child survivors after the war. He later went to America to train for the rabbinate, serving first in Bombay and New York and, from

1964, at the West London Synagogue, a post he held until his death in 1996. Hugo Gryn was committed not only to his own congregation, but also to the wider Jewish community and was engaged intensively in inter-religious dialogue. He was a regular radio broadcaster and appeared for many years on BBC Radio, notably as a panel member on *The Moral Maze*.

In the 1930s anti-Semitism increasingly restricted the life of Jewish families like the Gryns. His parents made plans for the family to escape from Europe, but loyalty to their own parents prevented them from putting those into operation. In 1938 Hungarian troops moved into Berehovo, soon followed by the German army. In 1944 the Jewish community was forced into a ghetto and later deported to Auschwitz. Hugo and his mother survived but his brother and father both perished.

Separated from his mother and brother on arrival, Hugo and his father were used as slave labourers. After liberation, he returned home to find a town whose once vibrant Jewish community had been destroyed, a town where there remained only 'a small handful of survivors, dispirited, most of them waiting in vain for the return of other members of their families'.

In 1951, while training in Cincinnati to become a rabbi, Gryn started writing about his experiences in the camps. The pages were discovered in a desk by his daughter Naomi after his death. His account of daily life at Auschwitz and later camps has great descriptive clarity – and is all the more shocking for that. He described the time when he found himself at the 'bakery' at Auschwitz (he assumed it was a bakery because the building had a tall, smoking chimney), caught up in a group of young children preparing to be 'showered'. Hugo was sent away by a guard but not before one child, walking naked through the double doors into the dry-floored 'shower rooms', recognized him and waved.

Gryn survived the concentration camps and devoted himself to community leadership. He regularly mentioned the Jewish spirit and the religious requirement not to give in to apathy or brutalization. He recalled what his father – who died in his arms just days after their liberation – told him in the camps: 'You and I had to go once for over a week without proper food and another time almost three days without water, but you cannot live for three minutes without hope.'

Hugo Gryn drew a message for people in all times and places: 'No one is safe when religious or ethnic prejudice is tolerated, when racism is rife and when decent, well-meaning people keep quiet because it is prudent.'

Golda Meir

Peace will come when the Arabs love their children more than they hate us.

Golda Meir was the Iron Lady of Israeli politics years before the epithet was coined for Margaret Thatcher. David Ben Gurion once described her as 'the only man in the Cabinet'.

She was born in Kiev in 1898 and emigrated to the United States of America in 1906 with her family. Her childhood memories of pogroms and anti-Jewish massacres during the 1905 Revolution led her to embrace Zionism and at school she joined *Poalei Zion* (Workers of Zion). She became a socialist and, after emigrating to Palestine in 1921 with her husband, was active in the trade union movement (*Histadrut*) and lived on a kibbutz. Later, she worked for the Jewish Agency, which organized the migration of Jews to Palestine.

In 1947 with the War of Independence approaching, she made two major foreign trips. First, she visited the USA and successfully enlisted the widespread support of American Jewry for the incipient Jewish state; second, disguising herself as an Arab woman, she secretly crossed the border into Transjordan and held covert talks with King Abdullah, trying unsuccessfully to persuade him to keep his country out of the war.

In 1949, a year after the creation of the State of Israel, Golda Meir was appointed Israel's first ambassador to Moscow and in 1956 she became foreign minister, a post she held for ten years. As such, she was the architect of Israel's attempt to create bridges to the emerging independent countries of Africa and fostered extensive bilateral relations with Latin American countries. She also endeavoured to cement relations with the USA.

Meir was a formidable woman: in appearance she was austere and in personality she was single-minded. In many ways, she personified the Israeli spirit. After the death of Levi Eshkol in 1969, she was called out of retirement to become the new prime minister of Israel, the world's third female prime minister (after Sirimavo Bandaranaike of Sri Lanka and Indira Gandhi of India). She was seventy years old.

This was the high point of a long career dedicated to the cause of the Labour party's vision of Zionism. When Golda Meir became prime minister, Israel was brimming with confidence following the Six Day War of 1967. She saw no need to seek compromise with the Palestinians so long as Israel was secure. Her concept of Israel was as a focus for the Jewish people throughout the world, exemplified by her dramatic expressions of solidarity with Soviet Jews who, facing significant obstacles and discrimination, engaged in an open struggle to settle in Israel.

Nevertheless, her government was plagued by internal squabbles, and a general lack of leadership. During her premiership eleven Israeli athletes were murdered by terrorists at the

Summer Olympics of 1972. She consequently authorised Mossad, the Israeli Secret Service, to kill those responsible wherever they could be found (hence the plot for the 2005 Steven Spielberg film, *Munich*). At that time she told the Israeli parliament, the Knesset, 'We have no choice but to strike at the terrorist organizations wherever we can reach them. That is our obligation to us and to peace. We shall fulfil that obligation undauntedly.'

Israel's euphoria was also punctured by the 1973 Yom Kippur War, which broke out with a coordinated Egyptian and Syrian attack. After early reverses, Israel – with American assistance – fought back, forcing Egypt and Syria to agree to negotiations. However, the government was severely criticized for erring in its assessment of Arab intentions. Much of the blame was directed at Israel's prime minister. The Labour Party won elections held shortly after the war, but Golda Meir, still facing criticism, resigned a few months later and was succeeded by Yitzhak Rabin. She died in 1978.

Jonathan Sacks

> After the collapse of Babel, the first global project, God calls on one man, Abraham, one woman, Sarah, and says 'Be different.' In fact, the word 'holy' in the Hebrew Bible, *kadosh*, actually means 'different, distinctive, set apart'. Why did God tell Abraham and Sarah to be different? To teach all of us the dignity of difference . . . The religious challenge is to find God's image in someone who is not in our image, in someone whose colour is different, whose culture is different, who speaks a different language, tells a different story, and worships God in a different way.
>
> (*Dignity of Difference*)

Jonathan Sacks, born in 1948, has been Chief Rabbi of the United Hebrew Congregations of the Commonwealth since 1991, the sixth incumbent since 1845. Widely recognized as one of the world's leading contemporary exponents of Judaism, the Chief Rabbi is both a scholar and spiritual leader of the British Jewish community.

He has spoken and written about ways for different cultures to live together, demonstrated by the subtitle of one of his books, *The Dignity of Difference: How to Avoid the Clash of Civilizations.* Sacks argues that in the past, the principles of religious tolerance or separation of church and state worked well inside the boundaries of a nation state. But today everything affects everything else, whether it is terror or economics. In response, Sacks suggests, difference should be not be viewed as a difficulty to be overcome, but as the very essence of life.

In Cambridge, he told my students the following: 'We are all different, and each of us has certain skills and lacks others. What I lack, you have, and what you lack, I have. Because we are all different we specialize, we trade, and we all gain. The economist David Ricardo put forward a fascinating proposition . . . This says that if you are better at making axe heads than fishing, and I am better at fishing than making axe heads, we gain by trade even if you're better than me at both fishing and making axe heads. You can be better than me at everything, and yet we still benefit if you specialize at what you're best at and I specialize at what I'm best at . . . every one of us has something unique to contribute, and by contributing we benefit not only ourselves but other people as well.'

Since religion is responsible for so much of the world's bloodshed, Sacks explains his views in religious language, turning to biblical stories shared by Judaism, Christianity and Islam. For example, he discusses the story of the Tower of Babel, when

God splits up humanity into a multiplicity of cultures and a diversity of languages. According to Sacks, God says, 'Be different, so as to teach humanity the dignity of difference.' Instead of the familiar notion of one God, one truth, one way, Sacks is claiming divine approval for human variety.

Sacks was criticized by some conservative members of the Jewish community for blurring distinctions between Judaism and other religions, and in particular for expressing the sense that God has spoken to people of all religions. The views he expressed in his book certainly went too far for ultra-orthodox Jews who argued that it was incompatible with Judaism to suggest the Jewish faith does not contain absolute, unique and exclusive truth.

Sacks refers to this experience as one of the hardest periods of his life but that 'some of the bad times were in retrospect the most valuable of all'. Although he amended some of the words in a second edition of the book (prompting an angry response from some liberal Jews who thought he had compromised too much), he looks back on the events of 2002 stating that 'in our interconnected world, we must learn to feel enlarged, not threatened, by difference'.

Andrea Rita Dworkin

> When asked how her Jewish background informed her feminist politics, Dworkin said 'When you are a minority in a majority culture, you have to learn to stick up for yourself.'

Andrea Dworkin, born in 1946, was a radical and controversial feminist who advocated resistance against sexism and anti-Semitism. She devoted her life to fighting what she considered the subordination of women, notably in marriage and pornography.

She was raised in New Jersey in a left-leaning working-class family and she credited her Jewish heritage, including relatives who were Holocaust survivors, for making her aware of human suffering and sexism. Her militancy she attributed to repeated readings of Ernesto 'Che' Guevara's *Guerrilla Warfare*.

Dworkin had a Conservative Jewish upbringing in Delaware. Although she loved Hebrew school and even received an award for her work, she did not have a *bat mitzvah*, because in those days, girls were not called to the Torah in the Conservative movement. As much as she loved learning, and Jewish learning specifically, there was no possibility of becoming a woman rabbi at that time. This prompted her leave Hebrew school and lead a secular life.

She commented that it was being told to sing the Christmas carol 'Silent Night' that led her to becoming an activist. 'I didn't think anyone could force me to sing it,' she said. Even when a Jewish teacher admonished her, telling her, 'I sing it; you can, too', Dworkin would not let the words cross her lips. Calling the teacher a 'turncoat Jew', Dworkin writes, 'It was my first experience with a female collaborator, or the first one that I remember.' The incident led to anti-Semitic graffiti being daubed on her schoolwork as well as a punishment from the teacher.

In her book, *Scapegoat*, she argued that both Jews and women are groups which have been victimized, drawing on examples from the Holocaust to illustrate this. In *The Jews, Israel, and Women's Liberation*, Dworkin wrote that 'violence born of anti-Semitism and from the hatred of women are similar'. She also argued that Zionism had turned Israel into a society of wife-beaters who feminized the Palestinians in order to oppress them. Unsurprisingly, she became an extremely controversial figure in the Jewish community.

Her militant lesbian brand of feminism also brought discord to the women's movement and she was described as a feminist version of Malcolm X. Famous for her outspoken positions on a range of issues from male-on-female violence, to rape and sexual intercourse, Dworkin's uncompromising stance brought fierce criticism not only from liberals, concerned at her attempts to pass laws against pornography, but also from feminists. 'I think that Hillary should shoot Bill and then President Gore should pardon her,' she wrote in early 1998, at the height of the Monica Lewinsky affair.

Andrea Dworkin is perhaps best described as a combination of an 'Old Testament Prophet' and feminist icon, someone onto whom a disproportionate amount of adulation and loathing is projected. Often in ill health, she died in 2005.

These five well-known Jewish figures illustrate that Jews can live their lives as Jews in many different ways. Each embraced Judaism as a part of their lives. The diversity of Jewish life is perhaps best illustrated by the following story:

> A Jew travels from Israel to the United States of America. When he returns, he tells his friend about some of the amazing things he has seen. 'I met a Jew who had grown up in a yeshiva and knew large sections of the Talmud by heart. I met a Jew who was an atheist. I met a Jew who owned a large business and I met a Jew who was an ardent communist.' 'So what's so strange?' the friend asks. 'America is a big country and millions of Jews live there.' 'You don't understand,' the man answers. 'It was the same Jew.'

6

What do Jews do?

The Synagogue

The word synagogue is derived from the Greek *synagoga* meaning 'to assemble'. As well as being a place of worship and prayer, it is a place of meeting and study, as is denoted by the Hebrew name *Bet Knesset*, 'house of meeting'. The synagogue is perhaps best described as a community building with a social as well as a religious function: a place which houses prayer, study and education, charitable work as well as social activity.

Every week on the Sabbath an argument starts in a synagogue, when the most important prayer in the Jewish liturgy, the Shema, is read. As soon as the first words, 'Hear, O Israel, the Lord is our God, the Lord is One' (Deuteronomy 6:4), are spoken, half of the congregation, who originate from one part of the Diaspora, stand up while the other half, who originate from somewhere else, remain seated. The people who are sitting shout 'sit down' to those who are standing while those who are standing shout 'stand up' to those who are sitting. The rabbi, unable to control the proceedings, visits one of the

founding members of the synagogue to seek his advice. 'Was it
originally the tradition for the community to stand during the
Shema?' the rabbi asks. 'No. That wasn't the tradition,' the
old man answers. 'Was it the tradition for the community to sit
during the Shema?' Again the old man answers, 'No.' The
rabbi sighs and explains his predicament. 'Every week in synagogue,' he says, 'the people who are standing shout at the
people who are sitting and the people sitting shout at the
people who are standing and . . .' 'Ah,' the old man interrupts
him, '*that* was the tradition.'

Synagogue buildings range from large purpose-built struc-
tures, to places of worship of other faiths which have been
adapted for Jewish use, or rooms inside private houses. They are
traditionally located within walking distance of Jewish homes as
driving on Shabbat is forbidden for Orthodox Jews.

The most important interior feature of the synagogue is the
'ark' (an acrostic of the Hebrew *Aron Kodesh*, which means literally 'holy cabinet'). It consists of a cupboard or recess in the wall,
which holds the Torah scrolls. The ark is generally located on the
side facing Jerusalem. Above the ark is located the *ner tamid*, the
eternal lamp, which symbolizes the commandment to keep a
light burning in the tabernacle outside the ark of the covenant.

In the Middle Ages in Christian Europe, synagogues were
located within the ghetto or Jewish Quarter (termed 'the Jewry'
in England where formal ghettos were never instituted). English
Jews often chose to live in proximity to the royal castle, where
they were subject to the protection of the Crown.

Synagogues existed in the Land of Israel and in Jewish communities beyond Israel during the Second Temple period
(536 BCE–70 CE). According to the Bible, Jews were expected to
make a pilgrimage to the Temple in Jerusalem three times a year,

though many, even those living in Israel, did not attend Temple that often. The earliest archaeological evidence for a synagogue is dated to the third century BCE in Egypt, and by the first century BCE it was a widespread institution in Israel and the Diaspora.

The synagogue as we know it today evolved primarily after the destruction of the Temple in 70 CE, though its plan and much of its symbolism derives from that original building. In rabbinic literature the synagogue is even referred to as the 'little Temple'. Some of the terms used in Temple services were taken over and transferred to the synagogue. For example, the Hebrew word *avodah* ('service'), which referred to service in the Temple (i.e. sacrifice), was replaced by service of the heart (i.e. prayer) in the synagogue.

Most importantly, the synagogue was a democratizing institution, for it brought Jewish worship within reach of every Jew, not only those who could visit the Temple. Since no sacrifices could take place in a synagogue, worship did not have to be conducted by priests. And, since sacrifices were replaced by prayer, the worshippers were able to participate rather than being mere spectators as they had been in the Temple.

As a House of Prayer, worship takes place primarily in Hebrew, although the prayer books are generally in Hebrew and the vernacular, say English (and at a Progressive synagogue the service is largely in the vernacular). Jews are expected to pray as individuals and as a family; and they are also expected to pray as a community. Indeed, certain prayers can only be said in the presence of a *minyan* (according to Orthodox Judaism, a quorum of ten adult men) and the traditional view exists that it is more beneficial to pray with a group than to pray alone. Men and women sit separately in Orthodox services but in Progressive synagogues all sit together. Men are required to cover their heads in both.

As a House of Study, the synagogue is a centre for the

analysis of Jewish texts, a life-long task. As Albert Einstein said, 'Wisdom is not a product of schooling but of the lifelong attempt to acquire it.' The synagogue normally includes a well-stocked library of books and is the place where children receive their basic religious education. In my synagogue, members of the community often meet an hour before services to study the weekly Torah reading. There are also regular classes in Hebrew (both biblical and modern) as well as classes for prospective converts to Judaism. It is also common for Orthodox synagogues to offer classes at which the Talmud and other Jewish texts can be studied. The most popular Talmud class I attended as a student was called 'lunch and learn with the rabbis'. Bagels and study complemented each other very well.

As a House of Meeting, the synagogue offers a social dimension for the community including both religious and non-religious activities. It often hosts, for example, clubs for the youth and also for the elderly, as well as social events for the congregants. The synagogue also functions as a social welfare agency, sometimes working closely with local churches, to collect and dispense money and other items of aid for the poor.

The synagogue is generally managed by a board of directors, or a council. No collection plates are passed around during services. Instead, synagogues are financed through annual membership fees and voluntary donations. The council is responsible for employing a rabbi for the community. But a synagogue can exist without a rabbi: religious services can be, and often are, conducted in whole or in part by lay people. Unlike leaders in many other faiths, a rabbi is not a priest and has no special religious status, as the following story intimates.

A rabbi has a heart attack and is confined to hospital for several weeks. One day the chairman of the synagogue council visits him and says, 'I want you to know, rabbi, that the council voted a resolution wishing you a speedy recovery.' The rabbi smiles in appreciation. The chairman continues, 'And it passed by twelve votes to nine.'

Prayer

A well-known rabbi and a taxi driver arrive together at the gates of Heaven. The angel at the gate signals to the taxi driver to enter, then turns to the rabbi and sadly shakes his head. 'What is this?' asks the rabbi. 'I am a learned rabbi and he is only a taxi driver who, not to put too fine a point on it, drove like a lunatic.' 'Exactly so,' replies the angel. 'When you spoke, people slept. But when they got into his taxi, believe me, they prayed!'

In Hebrew the verb 'to pray', *hitpallel*, literally means 'to work on oneself', demonstrating that prayer benefits the worshipper, rather than God. For Jews, prayer is an act of introspection and self-transformation. It is not magic, nor is it an attempt to bend the world to our will. If anything it does the opposite: it helps us to notice the things we otherwise take for granted. And seeing things differently, we may begin to act differently. Jewish prayer always begins with the praise of God and its imagery is that of the worshipper approaching God directly.

During the Babylonian exile, in the sixth century BCE, Jews were not able to perform sacrifices in the Temple, so prayer became a substitute for sacrifice. When the Bible commands Jews to serve God 'with all your heart', the rabbis were asked, 'What is service with all your heart?' They answered: 'It is prayer.' Or, as the prophet Hosea said, 'The offerings of our lips instead of bulls.'

Jews traditionally pray three times a day, corresponding to the three daily sacrifices held during Temple times. There is an additional prayer service on Shabbat and on certain holidays, corresponding to the additional sacrifices of those days. The basic unit of Jewish prayer is the blessing, which has the power to transform an everyday act into one that is an acknowledgement of God's role in the world.

Some prayers that were originally composed in biblical times are still used today, such as the Shema, which was recited by the Temple priests along with the Ten Commandments and various benedictions. Other prayers, such as the *Amidah* (which means 'standing' because Jews stand during its recital) were developed in the post-biblical period. This prayer is also called the *Shemoneh Esrei* (which means 'eighteen' and refers to the eighteen blessings originally contained within the prayer) and can be broken down into three categories: praising God, petitioning God, and thanking God.

As well as prayer the Jewish service includes teaching. This component of the service has also existed since early biblical times. For example, the prophet Isaiah describes how the people gathered in the Temple courts to receive instruction as well as to pray. In the Second Temple period, Nehemiah describes how Ezra recited and translated passages from the Pentateuch for the benefit of the whole community.

This practice continues today and a reading from the Written Torah (The Five Books of Moses) and from the Prophets (known as the Haftorah) are central features of the synagogue service. The Torah is divided into sections, so that if one section is read each week the Torah can be covered in a year. These are read on Mondays and Thursdays in Orthodox synagogues, and on Shabbat and some holidays in all synagogues. The Torah is paraded around the sanctuary before it is brought to rest on the *bimah* ('podium') and it is considered an honour to be called up to recite a blessing (called an *Aliyah*) over the reading.

The Torah was viewed by the rabbis as the source of freedom and goodness – and of life itself. It has even been described as pre-existent (similar, perhaps, to the Christian understanding of the Logos). God is sometimes portrayed as taking counsel with Torah – this is how some rabbis here interpreted Genesis 1:26 and the divine utterance, 'Let us make man.' On other occasions, the Torah has been described as the 'daughter of God' or the 'bride of Israel'. It has even been portrayed as pleading with God on behalf of Israel, particularly when Israel has sinned. In accepting the Torah, Israel differentiates itself from the other nations and becomes 'chosen'.

The Torah imposes on every Jew the duty to study God's teaching, which was interpreted to mean that public teaching of the Torah should be part of the synagogue liturgy. The Torah is not only read (or chanted in more traditional synagogues) in Hebrew but also translated into English. Even in biblical times, when Aramaic was spoken rather than Hebrew, the Torah was translated and these translations would generally include an element of interpretation.

There is, of course, a fine line between translation and interpretation. One favourite essay question for my students is: 'All translation is interpretation – Discuss.' The rabbis were aware of the difficulties of translation and commented, 'He who translates a verse with strict literalness is a falsifier and he who makes an addition to it a blasphemer.'

The reading of the Torah and the Haftorah is followed by a homily or sermon, often delivered by a rabbi. The story is told of two congregants comparing the sermons delivered by their respective rabbis. The first extols his rabbi, explaining how he can speak for an hour on any topic. His companion laughs and exclaims, 'This is nothing. My rabbi can speak for two hours on no topic.'

After the Torah service, the final prayers are said. They conclude with the mourners' prayer called the *kaddish*, which means sanctification. This prayer extols God and expresses hope for the establishment of God's kingdom on earth. It is recited at funerals as well as in synagogue. Children are expected to say kaddish for eleven months after the death of a parent and also on the anniversary of the death (called *yahrzeit*). In most synagogues it is customary to stand during the kaddish, although only the mourners themselves chant the prayer, while the rest of the congregation chant responsively.

Future Concerns

At the beginning of this book, I offered a threefold description of Jews as a religious community, a land-based people and a culture. In this closing section I will describe a major concern for the future of Judaism from each of these perspectives. I hope the reader will notice that each concern is relevant to all aspects of Jewish life today.

Encountering the Other: the concern from a religious perspective

> When a stranger lives with you in your land, do not ill-treat him. The stranger who lives with you shall be treated like a native-born. Love him as yourself for you were strangers in the land of Egypt. I am the Lord your God.
>
> (Leviticus 19:33–4)

For Jonathan Sacks, the command to love our neighbour impels Jews to embrace the 'dignity of difference' and to get to know people of other faiths and no faith, to meet them directly, and to share and expose our full religious consciousness to each other. This religious approach to inter-faith dialogue attempts to speak to the Other with a full respect of what the Other is and has to say.

In modern times three European Jewish thinkers, each active in inter-faith dialogue, have reflected upon this topic. Franz Rosenzweig argued that truth could exist in two forms, in Judaism and in Christianity. In 1913, after his close cousins Hans and Rudolf Ehrenberg and his friend Eugen Rosenstock had converted to Christianity, he likewise faced the decision of whether or not to be baptized. Before taking this step, he studied Judaism and participated in the High Holy Days services. He decided to remain a Jew and wrote to his cousin Rudolf to explain his decision: 'We agree upon the meaning of Christ and His Church in the world: no one comes to the Father except through him. No one *comes* to the Father – but it is different if one does not have to come to the Father because he or she *is* with Him already.'

Rosenzweig's famous response to John 14:6 ('No one can reach the Father except through me') introduces a crucial question for Jews in dialogue with Christians in particular and with other faiths in general. Jews expect Christians to view Judaism as a valid religion in its own terms and to reflect on the remarkable survival of the Jewish people and of the vitality of Judaism over 2,000 years. But questions also need to be considered in reverse. For example, what was the purpose behind the creation of Christianity? What is the significance of the fact that two billion Christians read the Jewish Bible? Does the fact that Jesus was a Jew have any implications for Jews? It is well known that we Jews are proud of famous figures such as Abraham, Moses, Hillel, Rashi, Maimonides and so on; yet Israel's most famous Jew, Jesus, is generally ignored. Now, in a climate notably freer as far as Jewish–Christian relations are concerned, is it not time that there was a greater Jewish interest in the Jew Jesus?

For Rosenzweig, the love of humans for God is realized in the love of one's neighbour. Redemption is the situation in which the 'I' learns to say 'you' to a 'him' or a 'her'. Jews and Christians have separate missions, but only together do they form the 'star of redemption' (the title of his famous book).

Rosenzweig was a significant influence on Martin Buber, who spoke of having a relationship with Jesus as an 'elder brother'. Pope John Paul II embraced much of Buber's theology, notably his description of God's covenant. During a visit to Germany in 1980, the pope stressed the meaning of dialogue as 'the meeting between the people of God of the Old Covenant, never revoked by God (cf. Romans 11:29), and that of the New Covenant'. In his prayer for forgiveness, left at the Western Wall of Jerusalem in March 2000, the pope called Jews the 'people of the Covenant'. In this papal recognition one can see the effect of Buber on Christian–Jewish dialogue.

In 1923 Buber published his major work, *I and Thou*, and began lecturing on Jewish philosophy and ethics at the University of Frankfurt. He actively supported German Jews who were being persecuted by the Nazis. In 1938 he emigrated to Jerusalem and was appointed professor of social philosophy at the Hebrew University.

In his exposition of the I–Thou relationship Buber maintained that a personal relationship with God is only truly personal when we are not overcome and overwhelmed in our relationship with God. This has implications for the human encounter – it means that two people must meet as two valid 'centres of interest'. Thus one should approach the Other with respect and restraint so that the validity of their position is in no sense belittled.

Finally and more recently, Jewish thinker Emmanuel Levinas searched for meaning in life in his work on time and love. Time, according to Levinas, is a function of the human relationship with another person. He said that time is 'the very relationship of the subject with the Other'. He acknowledged that the primary occupation of the individual is to take care of him- or herself. But this is not an invitation to selfishness. Rather, it is the fulfilment of a relationship with the Other. He believed that 'the existence of God is sacred history itself, the sacredness of man's relation to man through which God may pass'.

For Levinas, the face of the Other introduces and emphasizes ethical commitment. When people look at each other, they see not only two faces but also the faces of other people, the face of humanity. The relationship is more than 'I–thou', it is rather 'we–thou', entailing a responsibility for the other person. Levinas points out that 'there can be no "knowledge" of God separate from the relationship with human beings. The Other is the very focus of metaphysical truth and is indispensable for my relation with God.'

The continuity of Judaism: the concern from a secular perspective

Isaiah was in many ways a quintessential Jew. He warned Jews to be wary of those who believe they have the hold on truth. He also emphasized the values of liberty and pluralism, which show the way to a good life. His full name was Isaiah Berlin.

Secular Jews understand Judaism as the history, culture, civilization, ethical values and shared experiences of the Jewish people. Their connection to their heritage is found in the languages, literature, art, dance, music, food and celebrations of the Jewish people. It is not only – or even – religious beliefs that connect them to each other, but the entire civilization of their extended Jewish family.

An increasing number of Jews who identify themselves as non-religious face the same challenge as religious Jews: the need both to celebrate Jewish identity and to pass it on to the next generation.

There is a small but growing secular humanist movement in Israel that emphasizes the importance of the Jewish cultural tradition, from the Bible to Buber, in an effort to appeal to secular Israelis uninterested in religion. American humanist rabbi, Adam Chalom, has also taken up this challenge and has initiated a secular study of the Talmud. His online programme, entitled 'Not Your Father's Talmud', enables Jews to familiarize themselves with the Talmud from a humanist perspective. The website name, *www.apikorostalmud.blogspot.com*, a carefully chosen title, is derived from the Greek philosopher, Epicurus. For religious Jews, an *apikoros* is an agnostic or freethinker who denies divine justice and life after death.

The first humanist rabbi in Israel, Sivan Maas, was ordained in 2004. Her goal is for secular Jews to connect with each other and their heritage. She argues that Jewish tradition has always been an evolving enterprise, noting that the Hebrew term *Halacha*, Jewish law, is from the same root as the verb 'to walk'. 'When you're walking,' she says, 'you're changing all the time. It's only when the *Halacha* stopped walking that Judaism became irrelevant to many people. Or, if we're honest, to most people.'

In the last hundred years, many people have argued that the overriding challenge facing Jews has been to build the State of

Israel and to ensure its survival. It was an extraordinary challenge, to gather a people exiled for two thousand years, bring
them back to Israel and establish a sovereign state. During this
time, Jews managed to hold on to the dream of a Jewish state
even in the face of anti-Semitism and the Holocaust.

Today, anti-Semitism continues, and may even be growing. It
continues to create scars and wounds, which dominate much
Jewish thinking. At the same time, the Jewish people are widely
admired for their emphasis on family life, community support,
their contribution to charitable causes, and the priority they
place on education. They are admired for Jewish humour also:

> How odd
> of God
> to choose
> the Jews
> (Attributed to Hilaire Belloc)

> But not so odd
> As those who choose
> A Jewish God
> But spurn the Jews
> (a response by Cecil Browne)

> Not odd
> of God.
> Goyim
> Annoy 'im
> (a further response by Jewish author, Leo Rostein)

Nowadays, there is a pressing new challenge: the challenge of
Jewish continuity. From 1985–90, 57% of US Jews married

non-Jews. In Britain, during the same time period, 44% of Jews married non-Jews. How should non-Jewish partners be made to feel welcome? And Jewish continuity is not only a problem of the Diaspora. It is also a problem in Israel. While the Diaspora is experiencing an increase in mixed marriages and an increasing number of Jews dropping out of Judaism, Israel is experiencing the loss of Jewish knowledge and of Jewish values.

One response has been to increase the emphasis on Jewish education. Yet, although Jews are well known to value education, it is not enough that Jewish children go to Jewish schools. Education may bring knowledge, but it does not necessarily result in commitment. The greatest gift that Jews can give the next generation is to show them what they value.

If Jews have pride in Judaism, their children will as well. We must be proud to be what we are. The Jewish heritage is a rich one; it is a legacy well worth passing on.

Winning the peace: the concern of Israeli Jews

> Can these bones live? Thus says the Lord your God: ' Behold I will open your graves, and raise you from your graves, My people; and I will bring you home into the land of Israel . . . and I will put My spirit within you and you shall live.'
> (Ezekiel 17:3, 12, 14)

Much of Israel's history has been about winning wars in the face of great hostility. Israeli Jews are aware, however, that a successful future may depend on an even harder task: winning the peace.

Israel has won great military victories, none greater than the Six Day War in 1967 when the state appeared to be in a hope-

less situation. Under Arab pressure and with Arab armies mass-
ing, the UN peacekeeping forces left the Sinai Peninsula and the
Gulf of Aqaba was closed to Israeli shipping. Israel mobilised
and within a few days the situation was totally transformed. The
Israeli army heroically defended their country against appar-
ently overwhelming odds.

However, the qualities that win wars are not necessarily the
same qualities that win the peace. For one thing, winning wars
often results in a tendency to glorify military prowess, leading to
an unhealthy self-reliance and self-belief, bordering on arro-
gance. For another, war inevitably engenders enmity and
hatred, neither of which provides a foundation upon which
peace can be built. Palestinians living in the West Bank since
1967 have, for the most part, only experienced Israeli occupation and power. It is surely of little wonder that the attitudes of
many are so negative towards Israel.

Israelis are surely right to recognize that their country must
remain armed while there is the danger of renewed aggression
from neighbours or regional superpowers. Iran's threat in 2005
to 'remove Israel from the map of the world' serves to reinforce
this outlook. Israelis are possibly right to hold on to territorial
gains until wide-ranging peace is agreed; but in the end there
will be no security for Israel until mutual grievance is replaced
by mutual trust. To win the peace, Israel needs not only to
make territorial concessions, as it did by returning Sinai
to Egypt (1979) and by leaving Gaza (2005). It must also strive
to build bridges of understanding and friendship, between ordi-
nary Israelis and Palestinians, in particular, and Arabs, in
general.

For over half a century Israel has passed one military test after
another. Until fairly recently, Arab states did not want peace with
Israel. They rejected the partition plan of 1947 and for many

years denied the right of a Jewish state to exist at all. Some still do,
and the election victory of Hamas in 2006 is a sober reminder of
those days. However, the historic visit of Sadat to Israel in 1977
and the warm welcome he received from the Israeli public made
it clear that peace is a realistic possibility. Since then, there have
been sporadic outbursts of peace evidenced by the signing of
peace treaties with Jordan and the PLO.

There is no doubt that there are Arabs, whatever may have
been their past record, who genuinely desire peace. There are
others, of course, who still seek the destruction of the Jewish
state. Yet in the face of this ongoing hostility, Israelis need to
remember the courage of leaders like Anwar Sadat, who, like
Yitzhak Rabin, lost his life at the hands of a fellow countryman
because of his desire for peace.

If there is a desire for peace on both sides, the first condition of its attainment has been achieved. There is, however, a
second condition, which has been severely tested in recent
decades. Winning the peace requires compromise and concessions on all sides. This is not a call for pacifism. As William
Ralph Inge said, 'It is useless for the sheep to pass resolutions
in favour of vegetarianism while the wolf remains of a different opinion.'

At the root of the problem is a clash between two peoples
laying claim to the same land.

There were two brothers. Each owned half a field, but each
wanted the half he did not have and neither would give up his
half. They called in a rabbi known for his wisdom. He lay down
with his ear to the ground under a tree in the field and appeared
to fall asleep. After a time the brothers grew impatient, com-
plaining that the rabbi was wasting their time. But he told them
that he had been listening to the ground. It had told him that

neither of them owned the ground. It owned them. And one day, he said, they would be inside it.

The conflict will not be resolved in the long term by military means but only by political compromise and territorial concession. To an outsider it seems obvious what ought to happen – limited autonomy must evolve into independence and eventually into a federation of states, initially consisting of Israel, Palestine and Jordan, leading perhaps to an economic community of Middle Eastern States.

At some points in the future, morality and expediency will coincide and Israelis and Palestinians will have the opportunity to bring peace to the region. For Israelis, this will free Israel from the intolerable prospect of dominating an increasingly numerous and resentful Arab population in the West Bank. It is perhaps for this reason that Ariel Sharon ordered the evacuation from Gaza.

Some of the most vociferous critics of the Gaza withdrawal were strictly religious Israeli Jews, who felt forbidden to relinquish any of the occupied territories and opposed the peace process. They asked how religious Jews could support the peace process and give away land that God had promised. An opposing religious response, articulated by, amongst others, Chief Rabbi Jonathan Sacks, suggested that whilst it is a theoretical duty to occupy and retain this God-given land, in practice it must be given up, like any other commandment, before the overriding imperative of the saving of life. This is what is required to make peace.

It is in Israel's self-interest to make peace, as the vast of majority of Jews recognize. The State of Israel survived and flourished because it was able to withstand decades of attacks. It won the military battles. Its future survival now also depends on winning the peace.

Glossary

prepared by Rachel Davies

Aliyah: Hebrew 'ascent'. 1 Immigration to Israel, 2 Being called up to make a blessing over the Torah reading in synagogue.

Amidah: Hebrew 'standing'. Prayer recited three times a day; also called *Shemoneh Esrei*, 'eighteen' benedictions.

anti-Semitism: Hatred of Jews.

Aramaic: Ancient Semitic language spoken by Jews in late Second Temple period; main language of the Talmud.

Ashkenazi(m): Jews originating from Germany and Central and Eastern Europe.

bar/bat mitzvah: Hebrew 'son/daughter of the commandment'. Coming of age ceremony for males at the age of 13, and females at 12 or 13.

Charedi or see Ashkenazi(m): Hebrew 'fearful'. Strictly observant Jewish denomination; sometimes called 'ultra-orthodox'.

Chasid: Hebrew 'pious'. Refers to members of the movement founded by the Baal Shem Tov in eighteenth-century Poland.

Conservative Judaism: Non-fundamentalist denomination with emphasis on observance of tradition; also called *Masorti* ('tradition') Judaism.

Diaspora: Collective term for Jewish communities outside of the Land of Israel.

Galut: Hebrew 'exile'. See *Diaspora*.

Haftorah: Reading from the Prophets in the synagogue service on Shabbat and festivals.

Halakhah: Jewish Law from Hebrew root *halakh* 'walk'.

Haskalah: Hebrew 'enlightenment'. Jewish Enlightenment, contributing to Jewish emancipation in nineteenth-century Europe.

Israel: Hebrew 'struggle with God'. 1 People, nation of Israel, 2 Biblical land, 3 State of Israel, formed in 1948.

Kabbalah: Hebrew 'to receive'. Jewish mystical tradition.

Kashrut: Jewish dietary laws.

kibbutz: Collective agricultural settlement in Israel.

Liberal Judaism: Most radical modern denomination; *Halakhah* not seen as binding.

midrash: Hebrew 'search', 'enquiry', 'exposition', 'filling in of gaps in scriptural stories', 'deriving messages from them'.

minyan: Quorum of ten adult males required by Orthodox Judaism for public prayer or Torah reading.

Mishnah: Second-century text, first recording of the Oral Law.

mitzvah: Deed commanded by *Halakhah*; popularly refers to any good deed.

ner tamid: Eternal lamp symbolizes the commandment to keep a light burning in the tabernacle outside the Ark of the Covenant.

Orthodox Judaism: Traditional denomination of modern Judaism.

Rabbi: Hebrew *rav* 'great'. Refers to ancient sages or today, to someone ordained. Women can be rabbis in the Liberal, Reform and Conservative movements.

Reform Judaism: Liberal strand of modern Judaism; *Halakhah* not seen as binding.

Sephardi(m): Jews originating from Spain and North Africa.

Shabbat: Jewish Sabbath, from sundown on Friday to sundown on Saturday.

Shechina: Hebrew 'presence'. Immanent, female divine presence.

Shema: Most well-known prayer, recited twice a day, begins *Shema Yisrael*, 'Hear, O Israel'; from Deuteronomy 6:4–9.

Shoah: Hebrew 'destruction'. Preferred term for the Holocaust

shtetl: From Yiddish 'little town'. Now used in reference to the now-lost world of Eastern European Jewry.

synagogue: From Greek *synagoga* 'to assemble'. Jewish place of worship, study and meeting.

Talmud: Fifth-century compilation of rabbinic discussions; traditionally seen as authoritative.

Tanakh: Acronym of T-N-K, Torah, *Nevi'im* 'Prophets' and *Ketuvim* 'Writings'.

Torah: Written Torah refers to the Pentateuch; term can also mean the Oral Torah, the Talmud, and by extension religious teachings to the present day.

yeshiva: Primarily Orthodox institutes for study of Jewish writings.

Yiddish: Language historically spoken by Jews of Central and Eastern Europe; fusion primarily of German and Hebrew.

Jewish Calendar of Festivals

Month	Festival	Description
1st *Tishri*	*Rosh hashanah* 'Head of the Year'	New Year. Time of reflection.
10th *Tishri*	*Yom Kippur* 'Day of Atonement'	Day of Atonement. Time of fasting and repentance.
15th *Tishri*	*Sukkot* 'booths'	Autumn harvest festival. Commemorates temporary booths during Israelite wandering in desert.
22nd *Tishri*	*Shemini Atzeret* 'eighth day of gathering'	Marks end of Sukkot.
23rd *Tishri*	*Simchat Torah* 'rejoicing of the Torah'	Commemorates completion of annual reading of the Pentateuch.
25th *Kislev*	*Chanukah* 'dedication'	Winter festival of lights.

Month	Festival	Description
15th *Shevat*	*Tu-bishvat* '15th Shevat'	New Year for trees.
14th *Adar*	*Purim* 'lots'	Celebrates averted genocide as told in Esther.
15th *Nisan*	*Pesach* 'sacrificial lamb'	Spring festival to commemorate Exodus from Egypt.
27th *Nisan*	*Yom ha-Shoah v'HaGevurah* 'Day of Holocaust and Heroism'	Holocaust Remembrance Day.
4th *Iyar*	*Yom ha-Zikaron*	Day of Remembrance for Israel's fallen soldiers.
5th *Iyar*	*Yom ha-Atzmaut* 'Day of Independence'	Israel Independence Day.
6th *Sivan*	*Shavuot* 'weeks'	Spring festival commemorating the giving of the Torah to Moses at Sinai.
9th *Av*	*Tisha B'av* '9th Av'	Day of fasting and mourning for the destruction of both Temples and other atrocities.

Chronology

prepared by Rachel Davies

*c.*1800 BCE The Patriarchs and Matriarchs
Abraham, Isaac and Jacob; Sarah, Rebecca, Rachel and Leah

*c.*1300 BCE Exodus from Egypt
Lifetime of Moses

*c.*1200 BCE The Israelites migrate into Canaan

*c.*1020 BCE Saul
First king of Israel

*c.*1006 BCE King David
Jerusalem established as capital of Israel

*c.*965 BCE King Solomon
First Temple built

922 BCE Kingdom divided into two parts, Israel and Judah
Ten tribes of Israel, the northern kingdom, and two tribes, Judah and Benjamin, of the southern kingdom of Judah

721 BCE Israel falls to the Assyrians; northern tribes disappear

587 BCE First Temple destroyed; Babylonian exile

537 BCE Return to Jerusalem; lifetime of Ezra and Nehemiah; Second Temple built

*c.*200 BCE Septuagint (LXX)
Translation of the Pentateuch into Greek

165 BCE Maccabean rebellion against Greek rule of Antiochus Epiphanes

0 CE Time of Hillel, sage and rabbi; Jesus of Nazareth (*c.*4 BCE–*c.*29 CE)

66–73 CE Jewish revolt against Rome:

   Philo (*c.*20 BCE–40 CE), Jewish philosopher and classical author

   Josephus (*c.*37–100 CE), historian, author of Jewish Antiquities

   Fall of Masada in 73 CE; mass Jewish suicide in face of Roman army

70 CE Destruction of the Second Temple and the fall of Jerusalem

131 CE Hadrian renames Jerusalem 'Aelia Capitolina'
Temple to Jupiter built on site of the Jewish Temple; Jews forbidden to enter the city

132–5 CE Bar Kokhba revolt

200 Mishnah redacted by Judah haNasi

312 Constantine converts Roman Empire to Christianity

450–550 Jerusalem and Babylonian Talmuds finalized

638 Arab conquest of Jerusalem

900–1090 The Golden age of Jewish culture in Spain:

Ibn Ezra (*c.*1092–1167) grammarian and Bible commentator

Judah Halevi (*c.*1085–1141) poet

940 Saadia Gaon (882–942) compiles first Jewish prayer book

Rashi (1040–1105), commentator of Bible and Talmud

1095–1291 Crusades
Massacres of Jews in the Rhineland illustrating significant increase in Christian anti-Jewish prejudice and violence against Jews in medieval period

1135–1204 Maimonides
Rabbi, philosopher and physician; author of Mishneh Torah and Guide for the Perplexed

1290 Jews expelled from England

1306 Jews expelled from France

1488–1575 Josef Caro
Rabbi, author of Shulkhan Arukh

1472 Spanish Inquisition

1492 Expulsion of Jews from Spain

1497 Expulsion of Jews from Portugal
Jews migrate to Poland, Netherlands, Turkey, Arab lands, Palestine, South and Central America over the next hundred years

1516 Ghetto of Venice established

1567 Expulsion of Jews from Italy

1534–12 Isaac Luria
Develops Kabbalah, Jewish mysticism

1626–76 Shabbatai Zvi
Self-proclaimed Messiah (1665), converted to Islam (1656)

1656 Jews readmitted to England by Oliver Cromwell

1700–60 Ba'al Shem Tov
Founder of Hasidic Judaism

1729–86 Moses Mendelssohn
Enlightenment philosopher

1789 The French Revolution
Full rights granted to Jews in 1791

1791 Pale of Settlement created in Russia

1810 Reform movement begins in Germany

Abraham Geiger (1810–74), one of the founders of Reform Judaism

1837 Moses Montefiore (1784–1885), Anglo-Jewish leader and first Jew knighted by Queen Victoria

1858 Jews emancipated in England

1870–90 Aliyah to Israel aided by Edmond de Rothschild

Eliezer Ben-Yehuda (1858–1922) revives Hebrew as spoken language

1881–84, 1903–06, 1918–20 Three major waves of pogroms in Russia and Ukraine
Jews fleeing persecution emigrate, especially to USA and Palestine

1882–1903 The First Aliyah

1894–1906 Dreyfus Affair
Controversial trial and sentencing of Jewish captain, Alfred Dreyfus, exonerated in 1906

1897 Theodore Herzl writes *Der Judenstadt,* advocates Jewish homeland
First Zionist Congress held in Basel

1917 Balfour Declaration published stating official British support for 'the establishment of a Jewish National Home in Palestine'

1917 Pale of Settlement abolished

1920 British Mandate begins in Palestine

1933 Hitler comes to power in Germany

1935 Nuremberg Laws passed
Jews stripped of German citizenship and denied government employment

1938 Kristallnacht
'The night of broken glass'; pogrom throughout Germany; Jewish synagogues, businesses and homes destroyed and looted; 26,000 Jews arrested

1939–45 Second World War, and the Holocaust
6 million Jews murdered, 5 million others, including minority groups such as gypsies, homosexuals, Jehovah's Witnesses, communists and the disabled

1942 Council of Christians and Jews established in Great Britain

1947 United Nations votes for partition and the creation of Jewish and Arab states in Palestine

1948–55 David Ben-Gurion declares the State of Israel; Arab nations reject plan and invade Israel
War of Independence
Start of Palestinian refugee crisis

1948–55 Hundreds of thousands of Jews from Arab countries expelled

1964 Creation of the Palestinian Liberation Organisation (PLO)

1962–5 Vatican II

1965 Declaration of *Nostra Aetate*
Symbolizes rapprochement between Christians and Jews in second half of twentieth century

1967 Six Day War
Israel captures Jerusalem, West Bank, Gaza Strip, Sinai Peninsula and Golan Heights

1973 Yom Kippur War

1975 United Nations adopts resolution equating Zionism with racism
Rescinded in 1991

1976 Israel rescues hostages kidnapped and flown to Entebbe, Uganda

1978 Camp David Accord
Israeli–Egyptian negotiations; Israel–Egypt peace treaty signed in 1979; Sinai Peninsula returned to Egypt

1979 Pope John Paul II visits Auschwitz

1979–85 Operation Elijah, Operation Moses
Rescue of Ethiopian Jews to Israel

1982 The Lebanon War

1987–93 First Intifada
Palestinian uprising against Israel

1990s *c.*900,000 Soviet Jews emigrate to Israel

1993 Israel and PLO sign the Oslo Accords
Israeli–Palestinian agreement about steps to peace

1994 Vatican recognizes Israel

1994 Israel and Jordan sign peace treaty

1995 Yitzhak Rabin assassinated

2000 Pope John Paul II pilgrimage to Israel

2000 Israeli withdrawal from Lebanon

2000 Camp David summit
Israeli–Palestinian negotiations; no agreement reached

2000 al-Aqsa Intifada begins
Second Palestinian uprising

2000 Dabru Emet
Statement released by Jewish scholars on Jewish understanding of Christianity

2004 Death of Yasser Arafat

2005 Israeli withdrawal from Gaza

Bibliography

P. Alexander, *Textual Sources for the Study of Judaism* (Manchester: MUP) 1984

I. Bashevis Singer, *A Friend of Kafka: and Other Stories* (London: Penguin) 1979

M. Buber, *I and Thou* (New York: Scribner) 1958

A. Eban, *My Country: The Story of Modern Israel* (London: Weidenfeld and Nicolson) 1972

H. H. Donin, *To Pray as a Jew: A Guide to the Prayer Book and the Synagogue Service* (New York: Basic Books) 1980

E. Fackenheim, *To Mend the World: Foundations of Post-Holocaust Jewish Thought* (New York: Schocken) 1982 2nd edn

H. Gryn, *Chasing Shadows* (London: Penguin) 2001

A. J. Heschel, *God in Search of Man: A Philosophy of Judaism* (New York) 1956

S. Heschel, *On Being a Jewish Feminist: A Reader* (New York: Schocken) 1983

L. Jacobs, *A Tree of Life* (New York: OUP) 1984

—— *A Jewish Theology* (London: Darton, Longman and Todd) 1973

M. Kellner, *Must a Jew Believe Anything?* (London: Littman) 1999

N. de Lange, *An Introduction to Judaism* (Cambridge: CUP) 2000

P. Mendes-Flohr and J. Reinharz (eds), *The Jew in the Modern World: A Documentary History* (New York: OUP) 1995

D. Novak, *Jewish-Christian Dialogue: A Jewish Justification* (New York: OUP) 1989

H. M. Sachar, *The Course of Modern Jewish History* (New York: Vintage) 1990

J. Sacks, *The Dignity of Difference: How to Avoid the Clash of Civilizations* (London: Continuum) 2003

—— *The Politics of Hope* (London: Jonathan Cape) 1997

N. Solomon, *Judaism and World Religion* (London: Macmillan) 1991

G. Vermes, *The Changing Faces of Jesus* (London: Penguin) 2001

E. Wiesel, *Night* (London: Penguin) 1981

—— *Dawn* (Toronto: Bantam) 1982

Bible

A. Berlin and M. Z. Brettler (eds), *The Jewish Study Bible* (Oxford: OUP, New York) 2004

The JPS Torah Commentary Series:

N. Sarna (ed.) *Genesis* 1989

N. Sarna (ed.) *Exodus* 1991

B. A. Levine (ed.) *Leviticus* 1989

J. Milgrom (ed.) *Numbers* 1990

J. H. Tigay (ed.) *Deuteronomy* 1996

Dictionaries

L. Jacobs, *The Jewish religion: A Companion* (Oxford: OUP) 1995

R. J. Z. Werblowsky and G. Wigoder (eds), *The Oxford Dictionary of the Jewish Religion* (Oxford: OUP, New York) 1997

E. Kessler and N. Wenborn (eds), *A Dictionary of Jewish–Christian Relations* (Cambridge: CUP) 2005

Further reading

A. A. Cohen and P. Mendes-Flohr (eds), *Contemporary Jewish Thought* (London: Collier Macmillan) 1987

D. Cohn-Sherbok, *Holocaust Theology: A Reader* (Exeter: University of Exeter Press) 2002

H. P. Fry (ed.), *Christian-Jewish Dialogue: A Reader* (Exeter: University of Exeter) 1996

M. Gilbert, *Never Again: A History of the Holocaust* (London: HarperCollins) 2002

I. Greenberg, *The Jewish Way: Living the Holidays* (New York: Touchstone Books) 1993

Y. K. Halevi, *At the Entrance to the Garden of Eden: A Jew's Search for God with Christians and Muslims in the Holy Land* (New York: William Morrow) 2001

A. Hertzberg, *The Zionist Idea: A Historical Analysis and Reader* (New York: Harper and Row) 1966

J. Magonet, *A Rabbi's Bible* (London: SCM) 1991

A. Oz, *In the Land of Israel* (London: Chatto and Windus) 1983

C. Potok, *The Chosen* (London: Heinemann) 1966

R. Rubenstein and J. Roth, *Approaches to Auschwitz: Legacy of the Holocaust* (London: SCM) 1987

M. J. Wright, *Understanding Judaism* (Cambridge: Orchard Academic) 2003

Web resources

http://www.jewishvirtuallibrary.org
Jewish Virtual Library – General resource

http://eir.library.utoronto.ca/jewishhistory/
Academic Guide to Jewish History

http://sicsa.huji.ac.il/
The Vidal Sassoon International Center for the Study of Antisemitism

http://www.hum.huji.ac.il/dinur/
The Jewish History Resource Center

http://www.yadvashem.org/
Website of the Jewish People's Holocaust Memorial, Jerusalem

http://www.bh.org.il/
Beth Hatefutsoth – Museum of the Jewish People

http://www.imj.org.il/
The Israel Museum, Jerusalem

http://www.knesset.gov.il/index.html
The Knesset – the Israeli Parliament

http://nswas.com/
Neve Shalom – Wahat al-Salam – Israeli village established jointly by
Jews and Palestinian Arabs of Israeli citizenship

http://www.jewish-studies.com/
Academic Jewish Studies Internet Directory

http://www.jcrelations.net/
Insights and Issues in Jewish–Christian Relations

http://www.cjcr.cam.ac.uk
Centre for the Study of Jewish–Christian Relations, Cambridge, UK

http://www.clal.org/
The National Jewish Center for Learning and Leadership, USA

http://www.joi.org/
Jewish Outreach Institute

http://www.jrep.com/
The Jerusalem Report – Magazine

http://www.haaretz.com/
Left-wing Israeli newspaper

http://www.thejewishweek.com/
New York Jewish Community website

http://www.brandeis.edu/hrijw/
The Hadassah-Brandeis Institute – Judaism and Gender studies

http://www.fortunecity.com/exetershul/newsletter/poemspassover.
html
Passover poem

http://www.jewishvirtuallibrary.org/jsource/Holocaust/ccmap1.html
Major Concentration and Death Camps, Jewish Virtual Library

http://www.apikorostalmud.blogspot.com
Not Your Father's Talmud

http://www.lib.utexas.edu/Libs/PCL/Map_collection/middle_east.html
Maps of the Middle East

Index